MW00941914

There Is a River

Water: God's Magnificent Molecule

LARRY A. CARLSON

WESTBOW
PRESS®
A DIVISION OF THOMAS NELSON
& ZONDERVAN

Copyright © 2017 Larry A. Carlson.

All rights reserved. No part of this book may be used or reproduced by any means, graphic, electronic, or mechanical, including photocopying, recording, taping or by any information storage retrieval system without the written permission of the author except in the case of brief quotations embodied in critical articles and reviews.

WestBow Press books may be ordered through booksellers or by contacting:

WestBow Press
A Division of Thomas Nelson & Zondervan
1663 Liberty Drive
Bloomington, IN 47403
www.westbowpress.com
1 (866) 928-1240

Because of the dynamic nature of the Internet, any web addresses or links contained in this book may have changed since publication and may no longer be valid. The views expressed in this work are solely those of the author and do not necessarily reflect the views of the publisher, and the publisher hereby disclaims any responsibility for them.

Any people depicted in stock imagery provided by Thinkstock are models, and such images are being used for illustrative purposes only.
Certain stock imagery © Thinkstock.

Cover image by Tim Mansen.

ISBN: 978-1-9736-0059-6 (sc)
ISBN: 978-1-9736-0060-2 (hc)
ISBN: 978-1-9736-0058-9 (e)

Library of Congress Control Number: 2017912936

Print information available on the last page.

WestBow Press rev. date: 11/12/2018

Scripture taken from the New King James Version®. Copyright © 1982 by Thomas Nelson. Used by permission. All rights reserved.

Scripture quotations marked (NIV) are taken from the Holy Bible, New International Version®, NIV®. Copyright © 1973, 1978, 1984, 2011 by Biblica, Inc.™ Used by permission of Zondervan. All rights reserved worldwide. www.zondervan.com The "NIV" and "New International Version" are trademarks registered in the United States Patent and Trademark Office by Biblica, Inc.™

Scripture quotations marked (AMP) are taken from the Amplified Bible, Copyright © 1954, 1958, 1962, 1964, 1965, 1987 by The Lockman Foundation. Used by permission.

Scripture taken from the King James Version of the Bible.

Scripture quotations are taken from the Holy Bible, New Living Translation, copyright ©1996, 2004, 2007, 2013, 2015 by Tyndale House Foundation. Used by permission of Tyndale House Publishers, Inc., Carol Stream, Illinois 60188. All rights reserved.

The Holy Bible, English Standard Version® (ESV®) Copyright © 2001 by Crossway, a publishing ministry of Good News Publishers. All rights reserved. ESV® Text Edition: 2016

Scripture quotations marked RSV are taken from the Revised Standard Version of the Bible, copyright © 1946, 1952, 1971 by the Division of Christian Education of the National Council of the Churches of Christ in the USA. Used by permission.

Scripture quotations taken from the New American Standard Bible® (NASB), Copyright © 1960, 1962, 1963, 1968, 1971, 1972, 1973, 1975, 1977, 1995 by The Lockman Foundation. Used by permission. www.Lockman.org

Come, all you who are thirsty,
Come to the waters, you who have no money.

To
Mr. Alexander
Western Reformed Seminary
The Gideons International
Aquinas Academy Tacoma
All Who Thirst on the Pacific Crest Trail
"All Ye Who Thirst"
Cyber Dick Garrett
Punkaschöen
Bugs

Come, buy and eat!
Come, buy wine and milk without money and without cost.

CONTENTS

INTRODUCTION

"What is the PCT?"
"The what?"
"The PCT"
"It says 'PCT Crossing' on that sign back there."

I continued driving north from somewhere in Southern California while answering my wife's question.

"The PCT is the Pacific Crest Trail. It follows the mountains from the Mexican border to the Canadian border."

"Wow, we should walk that sometime!"

"Walk it? You don't walk the PCT. You survive it."

"How long is it?"

"About three thousand miles, I think."

"Wow, let's hike it!"

Why couldn't I get to be seventy years old and need hearing aids like other guys? Or I could have easily distracted her. "Hey, look quick. You'll miss the sasquatch over in that clearing." No, I had to answer the question and even stoke the interest. Or maybe I brought it all on myself when I took her down and back Grand Canyon afoot a year or so earlier.

Anyway, after four summers on the trail and a thousand miles on the boots, we are forty miles short of finishing Washington State, four hundred shy on Oregon, and about fifteen hundred short in California.

It says in Psalm 90 that the days of our lives are seventy years. Maudie and I are on God's extended warranty plan at halfway through our eighth decade. Though relatively sturdy, we occasionally return from a hike, with some understanding of the psalmist's warning, "With eighty years come only the boast of labor and sorrow." With that caution, it looks as if we should be grateful to finish the beautiful Pacific Northwest and look forward to an eternity of thanks. California would be great. But on the other hand, The Trail of Tears has already been done.

When you grow up and live your life in America, you have little opportunity to experience genuine worrisome thirst. When you hike the Pacific Crest Trail, recurrent thirst is built in. Often water holes are fifteen miles apart. Occasionally they are twenty. At eight pounds a gallon and in need of at least a couple a day in the desert, a backpacker is easily transformed into a sloshing, dripping human tanker. This book is, at its most divine level, driven by the Holy Spirit. At its carnal level, it owes everything to thirst.

Neither my wife nor I are big time on sports drinks, but when we staggered into Lake Morena, twenty miles north of Mexico, we eagerly downed a fresh strawberry quart of it offered by a generous camper. Record time. Later we reached Sheep Camp Spring, where we guzzled water streaming from its artesian source, a jet of aqua being pushed through the earth. We gulped it, we dunked in it, we spread it's cool, clear comfort down my beard and her locks. A short respite it was. We soon returned to lacing iodine into canteens filled from stagnant pools and to grubbing for water while hanging precipitously from the edge of river banks.

Sure, but what about *There Is a River?*

When one hikes up a steep hill gaining fifteen hundred feet in altitude in ninety-five-degree heat, hungry and thirsty, one may deal in some form of thought life. He or she certainly does not deal in conversation. If the thought life is positive and not self-destructive, and if the hiker is a Christian, it may turn to something like this. Well, at least it did for me.

"What's that verse about a river and a city?"

"Oh. There is a river."

"Right, then what?"

"There is a river whose streams shall make glad the city of God."

"Yeah, that's it!"

"But isn't the city of God Jerusalem?"

"Yeah."

"But there's no river in Jerusalem!"

"Well, that's true."

"Hey, Maudie, there's no river in Jerusalem."

"Huh!"

"There's no river in Jerusalem."

"You know, if you're going to hallucinate, why don't you write about it?"

There is a river
Whose streams shall make glad the city of God,
The holy place of the tabernacle of the most high.
(Psalm 46:4 New King James Version)

PART I

Creation to Condemnation

In the Beginning God

In the beginning God created the heavens and the earth. (Genesis 1:1 New King James Version)

Five-year-olds and philosophers alike have posed, in equal earnest, the question, "Where does all this come from?" Here's an entirely undocumented response from God; "I'm glad you asked that question. I'll start my book with the answer. It's a two-parter:"

1. In the beginning God
2. Created the heavens and the earth

In just four of those ten words the Singular, Eternal, Preexisting, Uncreated Being announces himself as just that. Singular, Eternal, Preexisting, and Uncreated. And like Forest Gump, he could just as well have added, "And that's all I have to say about that." Nonetheless, he has a universe of truths to disclose about what came, has come, and what is yet to come.

In the beginning God created the heavens and the earth. (Genesis 1:1 NKJV)

God breaks into world literature with an astonishing simple sentence. Noun: God. Verb: created. Objects of verb: the heavens and the earth.

"God." The noun to literally begin and end all nouns. In fact, he later identifies himself as "the alpha and omega" (beginning and end).

"Created." The verb to literally begin and end all verbs. The action word of all action words. This single word in its original language, Hebrew, is the act of causing that which did not previously exist to be existent. Only God creates from nothing. The best of our Edisons are not creators but accumulators and *temporary* culminators of previous inventions.

"The heavens and the earth." The objects of the verb to begin and end all objects of all verbs. Is there something more all inclusive than being the object of the verb "created out of nothing?" If so, tell it to the astronomer who explores the enormous or to the physicist who probes the infinitesimal.

> **The earth was without form and void;**
> **And darkness was upon the face of the deep.**
> **And the Spirit of God was hovering over the face**
> **of the waters. (Genesis 1:2) NKJV**

"In the beginning God created the heavens and the earth." God opens his book with ten words introducing himself as the Singular, Eternal, Preexisting, Uncreated Being, the One who created all that is from that which had never been.

For now the Rembrandt of creation has only two things to say about his canvas and oils and pigments. He will begin with darkness and as yet unshaped water. Amidst, under, over, and through this newly minted material his very Spirit "hovers." From this simplicity to the complexity of land, seas, moon, sun, stars, lichens, ferns, redwoods, amoebas, zebras, and humans, he has never stopped hovering. He never will. That is the page-by-page truth woven amidst, under, over, and through the remainder of his book, the Holy Bible.

> **Then God said, "Let there be light" and there
> was light. (Genesis 1:3 NKJV)**

Up to this point, only the creator fathoms the fathomless deep or the fathomless darkness. But the light show is about to begin. In the third verse of the Bible, the pitch dark theater is immersed in light. The projectionist rolls the film, a film he alone is able to view. His eternal name fills to overflowing the screen. "Producer "Director." "Screenwriter." "Special Effects." "Casting Agent." No "film editor" on these credits. No "take twos." All is "in the can" without flaw. And God will call the final product of every take "good."

Roll it! He is about to debut two previous unknowns. Light and water. Each will be his superstar over that yet to be created.

> **Then God said, "Let there be light" and there
> was light. (Genesis 1:3 NKJV)**

> Even as his waters remain shapeless, God illuminates
> them—along with everything else. Once again we don't
> get much detail. Merely all we need to know.
> God speaks, things happen.

"Then God said ..." God's shout blasted through the darkness. Maybe "shout" is a misguided presumption. A whisper is as good as a shout when you are the Almighty. In fact, the creator didn't actually require words. They are recorded for our benefit. He could have talked to himself; as a matter of fact, he did—apparently out loud. God orders himself to create the energy to run a universe. No sooner said than done. And there was light."

> **Then God said, "Let there be light" and there
> was light. (Genesis 1:3 NKJV)**

Many who have studied the matter (pun intended) now contend that the universe began with a big bang. It makes plenty of sense if only based on the first three verses of the Bible. If a mere cold front meeting an equally un-noteworthy warm front births deafening thunder, how much more of a racket would be created when total darkness collides with unrestrained illumination? And if a shrouded night horizon is turned to brilliance with one mass of sheet lightning, my, what a mornin' that first day's break must have been.

> **Then God said, "Let there be light" and there
> was light. (Genesis 1:3 NKJV)**

Now, about this matter of "light." Until recent generations, making light from darkness was a pretty big deal. That's one reason we celebrate the unknown prehistoric inventor of fire and the better-known Mr. Edison and his incandescent light bulb. Between the two innovations, our ancestors manufactured light only with considerable labor and expense. They bought and trimmed wicks, made candles, filled lanterns with whale oil, and hired lamp lighters. Even until the coming of America's Rural Electrification Administration in the 1930s and 1940s much of our nation ran on candle and lamp power. Do we who, like imitation gods, flick switches to turn night into day, even remotely appreciate God's first gift to the universe? We need to. It's fundamental. Light is the first fully wrapped present of creation. It is the monarch of physics. Its partner, water, is the king of chemistry. Absent either, there are no other gifts under the tree of creation.

> **And God saw the light, that it was good.
> (Genesis 1:4 NKJV)**

"Good?" A bit of an understatement, one would think. Imagine you invent a perpetual-motion machine for your high school science project. The teacher pats you on the head, issues a C on your report card, and blesses you with a "way to go!" Nonetheless, God is his own reviewer and critic, and he declares his initial project13 "good." Since nobody has come along to duplicate or exceed that first day's labor, we may assume that "consummate," "incomparable," "unsurpassed," and "matchless" are reasonable human synonyms for the divine understatement— "good."

Then God made two great lights:
The greater light to rule the day,
And the lesser light to rule the night.
He made the stars also.
God set them in the firmament of the heavens
To give light on the earth,
And to rule over the day and over the night,
And to divide the light from the darkness.
And God saw that it was good. (Genesis 1:16–18 NKJV)

Three times in this passage, sun, moon, and stars are described figuratively as rulers.

Rulers? Night and day are downright dictators! Weather, seedtime and harvest, gravity, calendars, tides. Night and day and their passage determine life itself. Ancient people around the world became dumbstruck by these great lights. So much so that they worshiped the lights rather than the lighter of all light. It's one form of what God calls idolatry. And that's another subject on which he will have very, very much to say.

And God said, "Let there be an expanse in the midst
of the waters, and let it separate the waters from the
waters." (Genesis 1:6 English Standard Version)

There is no weather to report at this point. But the ingredients are nearing completion. Light, darkness. The sun has been positioned perfectly in its celestial slot along with the moon. And now, on the second day of God's work, the "expanse" (sky) appears, separating the surface water from the clouds. All that is needed to justify a Weather Channel is earth, and that's on the next day's "to-do" list.

Then God said, "Let the waters under the heavens
be gathered together into one place,
and let the dry land appear" it was so.
And God called the dry land Earth,
and the gathering together of the waters He called Seas.

And God saw that it was good.
(Genesis 1:9–10 NKJV)

We may wish a little more detail about how the first cartographer mapped out dry land and water. We learn nothing of rivers, bays, gulf, estuaries, capes. No mention here of tectonic plates or even earthquakes or volcanoes. That, apparently, isn't God's objective at this point (or at any point) in his revelation of himself. In the coming creative days, he will disclose his labor in the creation of vegetation, animals, and humans. Each is succinctly declared "good." Here, even an attentive ten-year-old may well ask, "If it's so good, what went wrong?" And a yet more astute reader may add, "And why doesn't he do something about it?" They have stumbled into the apparent motivation for God's whole book.

> **The earth brought forth vegetation, plants yielding seed**
> **according to their own kinds, and trees bearing fruit**
> **in which is their seed, each according to its kind.**
> **And God saw that it was good.**
> **And there was evening and there was morning,**
> **the third day. And God said,**
> **"Let there be lights in the expanse of the heavens**
> **to separate the day from the night.**
> **And let them be for signs and for seasons,**
> **and for days and years,**
> **and let them be lights in the expanse of the heavens**
> **to give light upon the earth."**
> **And it was so. (Genesis 1:12–15 ESV)**

By the conclusion of day four, the creation parade has lengthened with the addition of the Botany Float and the Calendar Marchers. The grand marshal has made it so. As is becoming usual, all of this is pronounced "good." A latent biosphere of air, water, vegetation, and land now awaits day five. Its patience is rewarded in the form of a rich habitation of birds, fish, and more.

Then God said, "Let the waters abound with an abundance of living creatures, and let birds fly above the earth across the face of the firmament of the heavens."[1] In instant and obedient response sea and sky embrace fin and feather. The Zoology Float is mustered to formation.

> **So God created the great sea creatures**
> **and every living creature that moves,**
> **with which the waters swarm, according to their kinds,**
> **and every winged bird according to its kind.**
> **And God saw that it was good. (Genesis 1:21 NKJV)**

Here's that word *created* again. It debuted as the fifth word in the Bible and hasn't' been seen since. A review is in order. "In the beginning God created …" *Create* in this Hebrew form (*barah*) means the rendering of that which was absolutely nothing into that which is astonishingly something. God *barahs* sea life in such density as to be identified as "swarm." One has only to reminisce his or her first encounter with a swarm of bees, mosquitoes, or gnats to appreciate the word. Those waters were teeming with newly minted, first edition life. And you guessed it, "it was good."

> **God blessed them, saying, "Be fruitful and**
> **multiply, and fill the waters in the seas,**
> **and let birds multiply on the earth."**
> **(Genesis 1:22 NAU)**

To this point, God has communicated to the reader two concepts: (1) he made from nothing everything that is and that he did it merely by his verbal command, (2) It's all "good."

Now amazingly his first address, though brief, is to the animals. He talks to the animals, specifically to the denizens of his deep and his wild blue yonder. They are so "good" that he desires there be more of them. So many more that he chooses multiplication rather than addition as the mathematical process. God will have more to say about being fruitful and multiplying. But at this

---

[1] Genesis1:20.

point it may be well to contemplate that neither "conservation" nor "earth day" are ideas original to mortals.

Let Us Make Man

Then God said, "Let us make man ..." (Genesis 1:26 ESV)

Day six saw earth's population rounded out with land beasts of all sorts and a rather distinctive and unique co-occupant. Sky, sea, and land creatures had burst suddenly onto the planet, each collectively and without individual names. The creator's last entry arrives, like them, created from nothing (*barah*) but with his own God-given unique identity—man (Adam). And we soon find that the last hurrah is quite the *barah*. God is so satisfied with this act of production that he calls the labors of the sixth day *"very"* good.

Then God said, "Let us make man in our image, after our likeness. And let them have dominion over the fish of the sea and over the birds of the heavens and over the livestock and over all the earth and over every creeping thing that creeps on the earth." (Genesis 1:26 ESV)

Suddenly the Singular, Eternal, Preexisting, Uncreated Being hurls a dazzling curveball: "us." What's this "us" business? In what equation does "singular" = "us"? Answer: the pronoun *us* is here used in conjunction with God (*Eloheim*), a word which in Hebrew conveyed to the ancients an all-pervasive, overwhelming divine power and majesty that is implicit in God's very essence and being.

In our age, when powerful kings are only history and storybook figures, the imagery of royalty has become dim or lost altogether. Nonetheless, royalty in all its splendor and power *must* be here understood in order to begin comprehending the enormity and grandeur of the creator and his domain.

In the heyday of the British Empire, it was said that the "sun never sets on the Union Jack." (British flag). George II, the "royal we" of his day, reigned over the eighteenth century version of that massive empire. Yet when he heard the opening strains of the "Hallelujah Chorus" of Handel's *Messiah*, he rose to his feet. The audience stood with him—commoner, lord, and monarch—all in worshipful awe before the authentic "King of Kings" and "LORD of LORDs" whose endless banner is the universe itself.

> **Then God said, "Let us make man in our image, after our likeness.
> And let them have dominion over the fish of the sea and over the birds
> of the heavens and over the livestock and over all the earth and over
> every creeping thing that creeps on the earth." (Genesis 1:26 ESV)**

Curve ball one: "us." See proceeding for play by play. Curve ball two: "our image." So if God is so majestic and so powerful, just how is it that we are made in his image? One trip around the mall or gym, or even the Miss or Mr. America pageant belies that picture. So let's start with what "image" does *not* mean. It does not encompass the "omnis," which he has so clearly demonstrated in the first twenty-six verses of his book. "Omnipotent" (all powerful), "omniscient" (all-knowing), "omnipresent" (everywhere at once). We can't pass the physical. Oddly, he, himself can't even take one. His Word says, "God is *Spirit*, and those who worship him must worship in spirit and truth."[2]

It is in our God-given possession of relational virtues that we resemble the creator. Later we will learn that these include love, kindness, mercy, patience, endurance, generosity, and much more.[3]

For now we are only told that we are endowed with a benevolent, God-imaged relational potential of our own. And it is within this benevolent framework that God designed humans to rule over planet earth.

> **And God blessed them. And God said to them, "Be
> fruitful and multiply and fill the earth and subdue it,
> and have dominion over the fish of the sea and over the
> birds of the heavens and over every living thing that**

---

[2] John 4:24.
[3] See 1Corinthians 13, for instance.

moves on the earth." (Genesis 1:28 ESV)

For the second time, God issues a blessing post scripted with the command to "be fruitful and multiply." The first had come as a directive to the animal world, the second to man (Adam). Man's blessing and directive is tagged with an order to "rule" God's brand new teeming botanical garden and zoo. As deputy royalty, made in God's image, humans have been sublet dominion over the entirety of earth's life-forms. That's a daunting responsibility, then and now. The first of many God-given unmerited gifts. More will follow.

It is only man, among the millions of organisms walking, crawling, swimming, slithering, or flying on this planet, that can comprehend, internalize, acknowledge, and give thanks to the infinite blesser. What does God expect from the finite blessee in return for this amazing grace? Obedience! In the form not of grudging submission but of amazed gratitude. We'll see how well that goes.

God saw all that he had made, and it was very good.
And there was evening, and there was morning—
the sixth day.
(Genesis 1:31 New International Version)

The Singular, Eternal, Preexisting, Uncreated Being, once alone in eternity, is now immersed in resplendent and flawless company. And as the touches are finalized on his masterpiece, which we call the universe, he upgrades his evaluation from "good" to "very good." Since we all know it didn't exactly stay that way, he inspires the next couple chapters of Genesis with explanatory detail. Much of the specifics involve our primary subject matter—water. It too was "very good." So what's with floods, erosion, hail, blizzards, hurricanes, and droughts? We might ask again, "What went wrong?" Stay tuned.

And on the seventh day God ended His work
which He had done,
and He rested on the seventh day from all His work
which He had done.

Then God blessed the seventh day and sanctified it,
because in it He rested from all His work
which God had created and made.
This is the history of the heavens and the earth
when they were created, in the day that the
LORD God made the earth and the heavens.
(Genesis 2:2–4 NKJV)

Now comes a pause in the Genesis story. The LORD God takes time off and blesses his seventh day (Sabbath) to be permanently holy, set aside, and sanctified. Ironically, though production has officially ceased, he consecrates here his final gift of creation—rest. The history of creation is ended. The history of toil, sweat, and tears will soon begin. Never again, until the end of the story, will there be "rest" as it was intended in the beginning.[4]

The LORD God has a new subject in mind. He will dedicate an additional forty-nine chapters of Genesis and the remaining sixty-five Bible books over to the matter. And that matter is man and the LORD God's rocky, yet glorious, and victorious, relationship with him.

God's view of that relationship is so personal that he will, throughout scripture, identify it as *covenant*. The word conveys a contractual sense of commitment and oneness of purpose. And to emphasize precisely that, God tags, for the first time, "LORD" to his name. "LORD" connotes an unshared, out of time and place eternity, translating something close to "I am that I am." Yet this name is always used to emphasize God's special relationship to the crown of his creation—a soon to be tarnished headpiece.

No bush of the field was yet in the land
and no small plant of the field had yet sprung up—
for the LORD God had not caused it to rain on the land,
and there was no man to work the ground,

---

[4] Revelation 14:13 NKJV) Then I heard a voice from heaven saying to me, "Write:`Blessed *are* the dead who die in the LORD from now on.'" "Yes," says the Spirit, "that they may rest from their labors, and their works follow them."

and a mist was going up from the land and was
watering the whole face of the ground.
(Genesis 2:5–6 ESV)

One would think when watching TV weather broadcasts that *rain* is a dirty four-letter word to be dreaded on the level of the Black Plague. It is reported in dismay as a foreboding event and in glee when it is eclipsed by the sun. Notable exceptions occur during drought when the wet stuff is urged on and even implored. In the midst of a recent California drought, drivers even encountered off-road signs reading "Pray for Rain."

It turns out that the LORD God has quite a passionate and compassionate interest in rain and, in answering and, more often, anticipating that very prayer. At the same time as noted in this passage, rain was not his earliest and best medium for watering his thirsty world. "The LORD God had not yet sent *rain* to water the earth, and there were no people to cultivate the soil. Instead, springs came up from the ground and watered all the land."

No bush of the field was yet in the land
and no small plant of the field had yet sprung up—
for the LORD God had not caused it to rain on the land,
and there was no man to work the ground,
and a mist was going up from the land and was watering
the whole face of the ground. (Genesis 2:5–6 ESV)

Before there were fields and farms, before there were clouds and rain, there was the LORD God's wondrous underground soaking system. The thirsty earth was to be quenched in uniformly distributed H_2O, its faucet in the grasp of the master gardener.

Man is about to report to work. His job description: Work (cultivate, till) the ground.

Compensation: Eat fully and forever from the abundant variety of food the LORD God provides.

Working conditions: Perfect ground, perfectly fed and perfectly watered.

Perfect body.

Perfect labor force (about to be provided).

Six perfect days on, one perfect day off.

Vacation—you are on it. It's perfect. It's called Paradise.

Retirement—from what? You call this work?

In Hebrew, the "work" the LORD God performed translates out pleasantly as "occupation" or "business." Man's perfect "work" carries a different but gentle connotation as "till" or "cultivate." It will one day soon be described as toil."

Dust

**Then the LORD God formed man
of dust from the ground. (Genesis 2:7 NAU)**

As it turns out in scripture, the LORD God will have a lot of counsel for us humans about humility. He likes us to have it and to have it abundantly. We sort of get an idea of that intent from Genesis 2:7. Why not expand the account of our creation with a little self-esteem? Instead the LORD God details our biography by informing us that we are from dust. Dust! Why not a towering oak or majestic eagle? No! Dust! Amidst his most efficient primordial watering and ecosystem the LORD God left enough moistureless soil to assemble the first person. From dust!

On his part, this is a most impressive miracle since scientists tell us that we mortals consist of about 60 percent water. On our part it is cause for a pride-dispersing perspective. Give one of our artistic types a pile of Silly

Putty and expect wonders. Hand over a bushel of Dummy Dust. He will produce a pile of redistributed dust.

> **Then the LORD God formed man
> of dust from the ground,
> and breathed into his nostrils the breath of life;
> and man became a living being. (Genesis 2:7 NAU)**

Remember that self-esteem issue? It would seem the LORD God beat it out of us with the "dust" business. This is strictly a case of "read on," however. Check out the remainder of Genesis 2:7. The Bible is ultimately about good news. There's enough here for a Sunday Special Edition of the *New York Times*.

(1) "The LORD God … breathed into his nostrils the breath of life"—the Singular, Eternal, Preexisting, Uncreated Being initiates intimate contact with his prize product as he does no other. The human becomes God-breathed right from the start. Take a deep breath and feel the rejuvenation. If that heave of life is *rejuvenation* for you, then Adam's first inhale was *juvenation* itself. Sure, there is no such word. But just as surely there is nothing that explains the magnificence of human life than that it is, in its fullness and purity, the borrowed breath of the LORD God himself within us.

(2) "And man became a living being." "Being"—*Nephesh* in Hebrew. A soul. A God-breathed entity like no other. And what is it to seek self-esteem but to seek self-worth in and inside of one's self? How much more self-esteem could you ask for?

> Humans then, by DNA, and dictionary definition,
> are "God-breathed."
> No ordinary dustbins—we.

The LORD God Planted A Garden

**And the LORD God planted a garden in Eden
and out of the ground the LORD God made to spring up
every tree that is pleasant to the sight and good for food.
The LORD God took the man and put him in the
garden of Eden to work it and keep it.
(Genesis 2:8–9, 15 ESV)**

Here the Bible begins a recurring habit of representing the Singular, Eternal, Preexisting, Uncreated being in most human of terms. He "planted" a garden of trees. It veritably sprang from the flawlessly fertile soil. We are not told how the immortal, divine being plants. One can be sure it is not with bent back, sweat, grunts, and groans. We are just told enough to know that he is the first orchardist. And, as usual, his work is perfect. Each tree is eye-pleasing and palette-provoking.

With the garden now planted and thriving, he inaugurates the first "working" relationship. Man (Adam) is placed in the orchard to work and keep it. No added information on this either. Why would a perfect garden require weeding or pruning? Grafting is out of the question. Maybe Adam just harvested. In any case, one would safely assume God's crops are all of the "bumper" variety.

A River Flowed Out Of Eden

**A river flowed out of Eden to water the garden,
and there it divided and became four rivers.
(Genesis 2:10 ESV)**

In the pages of the Bible there are over one hundred references to rivers. It is astounding that this, the first, would be unnamed. Especially since there have been none like it since; a singular river that waters paradise, then branches into four other rivers. We are accustomed to tributaries joining to become one, not the opposite. Two of the branches remain obscure—the

Pishon and Gihon. The other two have repeatedly elbowed their way into history's headlines—the Tigris and Euphrates Rivers of the strife-ridden Middle East. These rivers, home to brutal empires, especially the Assyrian and Babylonian, will become associated in the Bible with foreboding, evil, conquest, and regret. The other great river of the Middle East, the Nile, fares no better. All literally and figuratively represent the domain of idolatry, captivity, enslavement, and despair for the people of God. In contrast, a baby brother among rivers, the humble Jordan, will be the watery standard for promise, hope, faithfulness, deliverance, and joy.

> **There is a river whose streams make glad the city of God,**
> **the holy place where the Most High dwells.**
> **(Psalm 46:4 NIV)**

Scripture makes liberal use of poetic, symbolic language to drive home profound theological principles and precepts. These truths often, but not solely, appear in the Bible's longest book, the Psalms, and involve water. Within the 150 psalms are poetry and song that capture the depth and complexity of the human soul and the power and the mercy of God. Here fly heavenward cries of adoration, perplexity, joy, and anguish. Here, also, the Singular, Eternal, Preexisting, Uncreated Being often portrays himself in decidedly comprehensible and earth-friendly images—many times related to water. In Psalm 23, he is the shepherd who leads his sheep to rest beside still waters. In Psalm 42, he is compared to a brook unto which the psalmist's thirsty soul pants. In Psalm 46 (above) he locates himself, as if an omnipresent being can be located, in the midst of a city beside a river— neither of which exist. Why? Because the Singular, Eternal, Preexisting, Uncreated Being desires that he be known and even loved (of all things) by fragile, mortal human beings. What kind of God thinks like this? Indeed!

> **There is a river whose streams make glad**
> **the city of God, the holy place**
> **where the Most High dwells.**
> **(Psalm 46:4 NIV)**

It isn't easy, once we catch onto the LORD God's "omnis"—*all knowing, everywhere present, all powerful*—to picture the "omni" LORD God physically dwelling in a literal city out of which a literal river flows and branches. Nor, in fact, does the LORD God desire such an idyllic, remote concept of his residence, essence or character. Instead, he seeks to convey in verses such as Psalm 46:4 his very self as the only source and citadel of true peace and joy.

It may be helpful at this point to know that the Psalms were inspired and written long ago, more than twenty-five hundred years past. They were penned, first and foremost, to an ancient people called the Hebrews (Jews). Prophets and poets alike strove to avert the hearts and minds of the Hebrews away from their earthbound fears, frustrations, and failures toward heavenly and soul-centered security in the safety of the eternal and everlasting LORD God himself.

These people, though dubbed as special and even "chosen" by God, often had reason to wonder where God was in their collective and individual lives and just what in the world he was thinking. More often than not, their lives floated on seas of despair, uncertainty, family strife, decaying social fabric, crime, injustice, economic failure, political discord, and even civil unrest.

Of course, individual, family, and national worlds like that no longer exist, and there is no reason to read on.

> **There is a river whose streams make glad the city of God,**
> **the holy place where the Most High dwells.**
> **God is within her, she will not fall;**
> **God will help her at break of day. (Psalm 46:4–5 NIV)**

Back again? That could mean, to quote *The Music Man*, "There's trouble in River City." Your River City. John's, Jane's Willie's, Amad's, Singh Rhee's, Thor's, Maria's, Red Feather's, Wong's. Every person has a River City. Every tribe and nation has a River City. And every one of their rivers has been polluted and wallows in desperate need of cleansing. Ancient Israel's capital, Jerusalem, home to the Hebrews (Jews), was no slacker in self-contamination. It often found itself nose deep in still cresting dirty rivers of slimy waters. In passages such as Psalm 46:4–5 the nation was thrown a lifeline secured to the pure waters and the unassailable city that is the LORD God himself. Hearkening back to the original streams of creation flowing from a pure, "very good" river, the verses beckon a drowning, soiled people to a paradise of body and soul.

> **There is a river whose streams make glad the city of God,**
> **the holy place where the Most High dwells.**
> **God is within her, she will not fall;**
> **God will help her at break of day. (Psalm 46:4–5 NIV)**

Is God just above it all in his ivory tower? Does he recline at ease under a sun umbrella on the warm, sandy beaches of his tranquil river? Is he unfeeling, untroubled, and uninterested as his omnipresent eyes gaze on my River City or on Toledo's or Nairobi's or London's or Calcutta's River City, or that of the ancient Hebrews? Or is he himself the city of refuge, safety, and trust as he implies above, or as he outright declares in Psalm 91:2? (New Living Translation)

> "This I declare about the LORD:
> He alone is my refuge, my place of safety;
> He is my God, and I trust him."

And is he more than merely the *Creator and Custodian* of pure waters? Is he, instead, the misery-defying, contamination- destroying purifier and restorer who is Living Water itself?

> **For my people have done two evil things:**
> **They have abandoned me—the fountain of living water.**
> **And they have dug for themselves cracked cisterns that**
> **can hold no water at all! (Jeremiah 2:13 NLT)**
> **God is our refuge and strength,**
> **an ever-present help in trouble.**
> **Therefore we will not fear, though the earth give way**
> **and the mountains fall into the heart of the sea.**

> Though its waters roar and foam
> and the mountains quake with their surging.
> There is a river whose streams make glad the city of God, the holy
> place where the Most High dwells. God is within her, she will not
> fall; God will help her at break of day. (Psalm 46:1–3 NIV)

Before the psalmist calls ancient singers and listeners to the serenity of the holy city and its pure stream (Psalm 46:4–5), he reminds them why both are needed. For some reason, their waters and their earth have become anything but a "very good" paradise garden. What happened? Back to Genesis, to the LORD God and his "very good" dustbin— "Adam" (man).

The LORD God Commanded

> And the LORD **God commanded the man, saying,**
> **"You may surely eat of every tree of the garden,**
> **but of the tree of the knowledge of good and evil**
> **you shall not eat,**
> **for in the day that you eat of it you shall surely die."**
> **Genesis 2:16–17 ESV)**

As usual, we get little detail on the only forbidden fruit in the orchard of trees "pleasant to the sight" and "good for food." All we know is that the "tree of the knowledge of good and evil," though likely very pleasing to the eye, was explicitly designated by the LORD God as off-limits to Adam's palate. In a seemingly generous exchange for this prohibition, the first human was granted dibs on any and all of the other delicacies. A most grand buffet. Yet not enough!

Any hurried driver at the 65 MPH sign or sugar-craving five-year-old in sight of a forbidden cookie jar can guess what happens next. No matter that the adult is transported, in one day, distances only achieved by his covered-wagon ancestors in months. No matter that the tyke is fed three squares a day, plus a snack or two and, perhaps, a dessert. All commands of "Don't" are trumped by impulses ranging from "It surely doesn't mean that" or "It really doesn't mean me," to "but, I need …" or "don't tell me what to do." If just this were not enough, Adam's neighborhood is about to be populated with peer pressure.

> **The LORD God said,**
> **"It is not good for the man to be alone.**
> **I will make a helper suitable for him." (Genesis 2:18 NIV)**

The LORD God provided, for the first human, plenty of companions, in the form of birds and beasts. He even brought them to Adam to be named. And when all that was done, he concluded that "companions" were not enough. "Companionship" was what was needed, and not one of the creatures qualified. God remedied the situation by providing the perfect "helper" out of Adam's very body. She was presented to Adam in the garden in the form of a full-grown girl formed from his rib. Adam named her generically "woman" and later honored her with the title "Eve," meaning "life" or "living," as the original mother of all humans to come.

So far, so "very good." It gets even better. The LORD God approved that first arrangement so much that he commanded it as the prototype for all to come.

> **"Therefore a man shall leave his father and his mother**
> **and hold fast to his wife,**
> **and they shall become one flesh." (Genesis 2:24 ESV)**
> **Now the serpent was more crafty than any other beast of the**
> **field that the LORD God had made. (Genesis 3:1 ESV)**

This is the first we hear of a cunning, deceiving reptile. He will be referenced throughout the Bible as actually a rebellious and fallen angelic being who makes it his business to be the ultimate enemy of both God and man. Scripture identifies him by many names including Satan, Lucifer, the Devil, Beelzebub, God of this age, Father of Lies, Murderer, Prince of the Power of the Air, Man of Sin, Wicked One, and the Tempter. Quite a resume—and nowhere near complete. He is also called a Roaring Lion and, by contrast, Angel of Light.

In his first biblical appearance in a leading role, the "Lion" moniker is apt. His roar is muted. But he clearly and convincingly dupes his first victims—Adam and Eve—in a subtle light show of deception. Consider the following, "Satan himself *masquerades* as an angel of light."[5] Read on.

> **Now the serpent was more crafty**
> **than any other beast of the field that**
> **the LORD God had made.**
> **He said to the woman,**
> **"Did God actually say,**
> **'You shall not eat of any tree in the garden'?"**
> **And the woman said … (Genesis 3:1–3 ESV)**

A bumper sticker of a past American decade read, "Question authority." It's plagiarized from Satan. He understood that rebellion is not birthed with swords and guns but conceived in confusion, uncertainty and doubt. A populace successfully implanted with these seeds is ripe for confrontation, challenge and outright insurrection. Satan, the founder and mastermind of revolution, templated the strategy in Eden. He began with confusion and uncertainty. "Did God actually say …?." He may just as well have said, "What is truth"? Before Eve bites the fruit, she first bites the bait, and eventually the dust. An uneven battle of wit ensues.

> **{Serpent :} "Did God actually say, 'You shall**
> **not eat of any tree in the garden?"**
> **{Woman:} "We may eat of the fruit of the trees**
> **in the garden, but God said,**
> **'You shall not eat of the fruit of the tree**
> **that is in the midst of the garden,**
> **neither shall you touch it.'" (Genesis 3:2–3 ESV)**

The woman appears to hold her own by restating the LORD God's prohibition. Eden's own memorization recital, or was it "show and tell, goes awry" when Eve adds to the LORD God's mandate. While not touching the

---

[5] 2Corinthians 11:14 (NIV).

tree of the knowledge of good and evil may have been a prudent precaution, it was never stated or demanded. Adding or subtracting words uttered by the Singular, Eternal, Preexisting, Uncreated being never proves prudent or productive. In this case, it is the first skid in mankind's slippery slope to disaster.

> {Eve:} "God said, 'You shall not eat of the fruit of
> the tree that is in the midst of the garden,
> neither shall you touch it, lest you die.'"
> {Satan}: But the serpent said to the woman,
> "You will not surely die." (Genesis 3:3–4 ESV)

The serpent knows that his opening salvos of "confront" and "confuse" have taken root. It's time for his "certainty" to displace Eve's uncertainty. He now offers for Eve's consideration the "big lie." Here he pioneers the staple of future con artists, smooth talkers, and dictators. Make your lie so huge and absurd as to defy rationality, discernment, or even common sense. Even misquote polemically the enemy's very words.

God: "You may surely eat of every tree of the garden, but of the tree of the knowledge of good and evil you shall not eat, for in the day that you eat of it *you shall surely die.*"

Serpent: "You will *not* surely die."

A little word, *not*. Yet, on these three letters hinge the door to all history.

> So when the woman saw that the tree was good for food,
> and that it was a delight to the eyes,
> and that the tree was to be desired to make one wise,
> she took of its fruit and ate,
> and she also gave some to her husband who was with her,
> And he ate. (Genesis 3:6 ESV)

Tasty! Beautiful! Profitable! No trespassing! It should be little surprise to we who have followed so faithfully in the footsteps of Adam and Eve that they found the *only* grass outside of true paradise to be greener than all inside. "No trespassing," posted on even the most formidable of fences, is but an inconvenient incentive when framed by "tasty," "beautiful," and "profitable" within.

A vote was held on that dark day in Paradise. Our mother, Eve, moved to elect a lie and a liar. Father Adam, though the original entrusted recipient of truth, seconded the motion. Motion carried. They ate. Their bodily and spiritual indigestion has become the bellyache of all subsequent human history.

> **At that moment their eyes were opened,**
> **And they suddenly felt shame at their nakedness.**
> **So they sewed fig leaves together to cover**
> **themselves. (Genesis 3:7 NLT)**

Certainly Adam and Eve, God's epitome of creation, already had open eyes. What are the eyes, then, that were opened for the first time? What did they see with their physical eyes that created, for the first time, spiritual eyes of shame? And who could they possibly be shamed before? What does a "real eye opener," as modern usage has it, look like? The English Puritan Matthew Henry explains it as follows:

"The eyes of their consciences were opened, and their hearts smote them for what they had done. Now, when it was too late, they saw the folly of eating forbidden fruit. They saw the happiness they had fallen from, and the misery they had fallen into. They saw a loving God provoked, his grace and favor forfeited, his likeness and image lost, dominion over the creatures gone. They saw their natures corrupted and depraved, and felt a disorder in their own spirits of which they had never before been conscious."

> **And He [LORD God] said, [to Adam]**
> **"Who told you that you were naked?**
> **Have you eaten from the tree that**
> **I commanded you not to eat from?"**
> **The man said, "The woman you put here with me—**

> She gave me some fruit from the tree, and
> I ate it." (Genesis 3:11–12 NIV)

There were two questions: Who told you, and did you eat the forbidden fruit? The family spokesman dodged the first and doctored the second.

Adam's Axiom #1: Skirt, evade, obscure, defend. Adam's axiom #2: When trapped, blame. Adam models victim mentality in a primitive but decidedly sophisticated form. Three shots at innocence. Blame "the woman" twice. Blame the master of the garden himself. After all, it was he who thought up and activated this whole companionship thing in the first place.

So much for "naked truth."

> Then the LORD God asked the woman,
> "What have you done?"
> "The serpent deceived me," she replied.
> "That's why I ate it." (Genesis 3:13 NLT)

Adam's opportunity for moral leadership of Eve is squandered in the forbidden fruit affair. He has given Eve no role model for courage in the face of failure. Role model for failure in the face of failure, however? She has learned that well.

Eve eventually concludes her defense with "guilty as charged." "I ate it." No obscurity there. But the confession is preceded first by transfer of guilt. "I may have been gullible," she seems to imply with the word "deceived," "but it was the serpent's fault." The comedian Flip Wilson enhanced much of his prosperous career smirking the line, "The devil made me do it." Plagiarism!

Dust, Pain, Labor And Sweat

> The LORD God said to the serpent,
> "Because you have done this,
> cursed are you above all livestock

and above all beasts of the field;
on your belly you shall go,
and dust you shall eat all the days of your life."
(Genesis 3:14 ESV)

The LORD God gives the deceiver no opportunity for defense. He immediately passes sentence.

It's a two-parter. In the first, the downfallen, rebellious spiritual being is cursed to a contemptible existence. He is, heretofore, the lowest of the low. The ruling is an object lesson in the adage "the punishment should fit the crime." Having impersonated a slithering creature of the soil, he will now in actuality occupy the rank of loathsome of the loathsome, aberrant of the aberrant, and repugnant of the repugnant. The fertile dirt of the garden, for the serpent, is replaced by the waterless spiritual dust of condemnation and despair.

The LORD God said to the serpent,
"Because you have done this,
cursed are you above all livestock
and above all beasts of the field;
on your belly you shall go,
and dust you shall eat all the days of your life.
I will put enmity between you and the woman,
and between your offspring and her offspring;
he shall bruise your head,
and you shall bruise his heel."
(Genesis 3:14–15 ESV)

Here the LORD God informs Satan that his victory over humanity and Paradise is momentary. Not only will he exist in degradation, but he is divinely destined for defeat. This is war. And the Singular, Eternal, Preexisting, Uncreated Being, the One who created all that is from that which had never been, now proclaims his sovereignty over the battles and the battlers.

Out of the adversary's spiritual seed will issue more rebellion and deceit. Out of the woman's womb will proceed a descendancy of human beings mired in conflict with the ancient enemy. The great Battle of Paradise has been lost by Adam's unconditional surrender to Satan. The gauntlet is down. The LORD God has thrown it. There will be yet another battle. This time to the death. Out of the seed of Eve will emerge the champion. Though bruised at the heel from the serpent's waterless, dusty lunge, the savior, "Living Water,"[6] will deliver a death blow to his head.

> **Then he said to the woman,**
> **"I will sharpen the pain of your pregnancy,**
> **and in pain you will give birth." (Genesis 3:16 NLT)**

We aren't told what childbirth would have been like had all stayed "very good." We only know that the most precious and satisfying of all female privileges, that of hosting and nurturing new life in and out of her very body, is to be accomplished in expanded and contracted suffering. Something has gone drastically wrong in Paradise. Adam and Eve have trespassed. They have violated their Creator and his creation. They have dishonored his glory, disrespected his generosity, and dismissed his authority. And for what? To possess and devour that which was the only no-no in a paradise of yes-yes. Trespassing against the LORD God will heretofore be identified as "sin." And it is sin and its companions—pain, heartache, guilt, and alienation— that Adam and Eve will pass on as genetic ingredients residing in all their vast family to come.

> **Then he said to the woman,**
> **"I will sharpen the pain of your pregnancy,**
> **and in pain you will give birth." (Genesis 3:16 NLT)**

God's judgment on his archenemy, Satan, comes without mercy. The serpent's doom must be sure and complete.[7] He must be forever hope*less* if Eves and Adams to come are be hope-*filled*. In childbirth, Eve and all future

---

[6] John 4:9–14.
[7] "A Mighty Fortress is our God." Hymn by Martin Luther.

expectant moms will incubate a roomful of hope and anticipation, of which only half of earth's population will even begin to comprehend.

Undeserved mercy in the face of judgment for sin! This will be a hallmark of God's love for his fallen creation. And water? Satan, doomed to spiritual thirst and dehydration, must forever slither in waterless dust. By contrast, woman's ultimate glory, her baby, will be bathed and protected in watery amniotic fluid. For nine months, having been a veritable blanket of insulation and warmth for the embryo, that water now bursts, discharging, in relieved glory and awe, its restless napper into the light of day.

> **Then he said to the woman ...**
> **"you will desire to control your husband,**
> **but he will rule over you." (Genesis 3:16 NLT)**

Much later in the Bible, Jesus Christ, the champion and savior predicted in Genesis 3:15, will announce to his followers that "where two or three are gathered in my name, there am I also." (Matthew 18:20). The verse is recorded as central in his formula for conflict resolution. For now, here in the rapidly disintegrating paradise, interpersonal struggle is virtually guaranteed when merely two are gathered together. And it will be first found and played out within the sacred boundaries of God- ordained matrimony.

The harmony of Eden's song is being fully replaced by the abrasive dissonant chords of rejection and separation. Man's sudden disintegrated relationship with God is partnered by discord within his very own once perfectly integrated being. Adam has sacrificed, on the altar of greed, his own harmony with himself. Life is replaced with death. Health is displaced by pain. Further, Adam is now out of harmony and relationship with Eve. With envy, partisanship, and power struggle the new reality in man's relationship with man, inter-human harmony draws to a tragic close.[8]

---

[8] The concept of man's harmony with God, himself, others, and with nature being replaced by disharmony with all four is taken from the Bethel Bible Series. *The Bethel Series*, Copyright 1961, 1981, 2000, 2011 by The Adult Christian Education Foundation, Inc., Waunakee, WI, all rights reserved.

> And to Adam He said,
> Because you have listened to the voice of your wife
> and have eaten of the tree of which I commanded you,
> "You shall not eat of it,"
> cursed is the ground because of you;
> in pain you shall eat of it all the days of your life;
> thorns and thistles it shall bring forth for you;
> and you shall eat the plants of the field.
> (Genesis 3:17–18 ESV)

Nature gets no special treatment. It too is cursed. A most discordant quartet of disharmony is now rounded out. Adam is out of harmony with the LORD God, with himself, with others, and now with the formerly "good" earth.

Just as Adam will face a struggle for life and the certainty of eventual death, so his crops will gasp for breath among the tangle of thorns and thistles. Just as his wife will face pain and sorrow in producing the fruit of the womb, so he must endure pain and sorrow in cultivating and gathering sustenance for his family. Earth's first man, once privileged to stand on two feet gleaning the flawless crop of Eden's fruit orchard, must now crouch on his haunches and stoop to his knees to sow, cultivate, and harvest from a hostile earth, a planet which was once his friend.

> By the sweat of your brow
> you will eat your food until you return to the ground,
> since from it you were taken;
> for dust you are and to dust you will return.
> (Genesis 3:19 NIV)

For each of Eden's three vanquished insurrectionists, a judgment is pronounced that incorporates water. To the serpent—an eternity of belly-down waterless eating of dust. To the woman—a watery sheath of protection for her and her child as she endures the pain of pregnancy, labor and childbirth.

As for the man—pain and sweat in the tedious and laborious toil of farming. But again there is an upside. As water mitigates Eve's pain, so Adam's sweat will enable his stressed body thermostat to retain stability in the midst of heat and exertion. One last water reference remains. Man, the H_2O fortified dustbin, must return to the waterless dusty state from which he came. He must, contrary to Satan's cynical assurance, die! From "dust you were taken; for dust you are and to dust you will return."

The creation account now draws dismally to a twofold closure. 1. With death an apparent and irreversible certainty, he [God] drove out the man. 2. "At the east of the Garden of Eden he placed the cherubim [angels] and a flaming sword that turned every way to guard the way to the tree of life."[9] No admittance. No trespassing.

The Word

In the beginning was the Word,
And the Word was with God, and the Word was God.
He was in the beginning with God.
All things were made through him,
And without him was not anything made
that was made. (John 1:1 ESV)

So where is the champion and savior of Genesis 3:15? The Bible pours out about two thousand more pages before it concludes and resolves in a fully restored and redeemed universe. The thirty nine books of its Old Testament all point prophetically toward him. The four Gospel (Good News)[10] books of the New Testament point biographically at him. The twenty-three remaining New Testament books point reflectively back at him. Jesus Christ, the Word, the Son of God, is the Bible's "grand subject, our good the design, and the glory of God its end."[11]

---

[9] Genesis 3:24.

[10] Translations from Greek of the New Testament's word *euaggelizo* are rendered into English as "Gospel" or "Good News."

[11] *Introduction to Bibles* distributed by Gideon International.

> **And the Word became flesh and dwelt among us,**
> **and we have seen his glory,**
> **glory as of the only Son from the Father,**
> **full of grace and truth.**
> **(John 1:14 ESV)**

The Singular, Eternal, Preexisting, Uncreated Being, the master gardener of Eden and its judge, is that very Genesis 3:15 champion and savior. He, in love so divine as to defy comprehension, left heavenly eternity, and broke humbly into human history as a lowly baby. He lived, died, was resurrected bodily, and ascended to heavenly glory to restore the certain hope of life to a lost and condemned creation. His is the story of all stories. He is the only happily ever after" alternative to a factual "once upon a time" gone desperately wrong.

> **A woman, when she is in labor,**
> **has sorrow because her hour has come;**
> **but as soon as she has given birth to the child,**
> **she no longer remembers the anguish,**
> **for joy that a human being has been born into**
> **the world. (John 16:21 NKJV)**

When Jesus Christ, the Word, "became flesh and dwelt among us" two thousand years ago, he never forgot the penalties imposed upon Adam, Eve, and their progeny. In this passage, he references the woman's travail in childbirth. The anguish of physical pain grieves and sorrows her. But it will very soon give way to the relief and joy of liberating, bursting water.

Here he is speaking to his eleven disciples. Minutes before, there were twelve. One has gone on his mission to betray Jesus. The Son of God himself, that very night, will be taken away to be condemned by religious leaders. One daybreak separates him from torturous, excruciating death by Roman crucifixion. By nightfall he will be entombed. What joy can flood from that trauma?

> A woman, when she is in labor,
> has sorrow because her hour has come;
> but as soon as she has given birth to the child,
> she no longer remembers the anguish,
> for joy that a human being has been born into
> the world. (John 16:21 NKJV)

What could the childbirth illustration possibly convey to the eleven anxious males on that momentous evening? In the close family proximities of first century AD Jerusalem and its environs, the sights and sounds of delivery were well known by all. Perhaps, more likely than not, most of them had witnessed the process. No painkillers, no birthing beds, no insulated walls—if walls at all. They likely remembered the water. They certainly remembered the grimaces, the clutching, the gasping, and the screams. They remembered the restored respiration, the smiles. And they remembered most of all the joy, individual and communal, of a human being ... born into the world.

> A woman, when she is in labor,
> has sorrow because her hour has come;
> but as soon as she has given birth to the child,
> she no longer remembers the anguish,
> for joy that a human being has been born into
> the world. (John 16:21 NKJV)

Jesus certainly parallels a woman's travail in the suffering he is about to encounter. But where's the joy? Where's the new life? Does the analogy break down? It's Thursday. By dusk on Friday, Jesus will be dead and buried. No funeral service. No obituary. No preacher, no eulogy or kind and homey remembrances by friends. Just disgrace, dishonor, and defeat. A lot like Eden. But worse, much worse. This time the champion, the savior, the last chance, the second Adam, is dead. And what of Saturday? A huge boulder and a detail of soldiers guard his tomb from potential grave robbing by his followers.

Not enough! It is Sunday daybreak, and the tomb is empty. The champion and savior, the Son of God and Second Adam, has burst its bounds. He has risen! The new baby is once and forever born. Her name is Joy. She is the Joy of death defeated. She is the Joy of bodily resurrection from the dead. She is the Joy of curse lifted. She is the Joy of harmony restored. She is the Joy of eternal life available. She is the Joy of victory. Just as forecast, the woman's seed has vanquished the ancient foe. What a terrible bruising the Son of God's heel has taken![12]

What a mortally decisive blow has been sledge hammered deep to the serpent's sorry head. Joy in the morning!

> **By the sweat of your brow**
> **you will eat your food until you return to the ground,**
> **since from it you were taken;**
> **for dust you are and to dust you will return.**
> **(Genesis 3:19 NIV)**

Sweat is a benevolent function providing life-supportive heating and cooling. Such knowledge provides little consolation to toiling sons of Adam who wearily drip of the salty brine. Neither does the realization that the dust he moistens may be calling, "This could be you."

In this Genesis curse is the first of only three Bible citings of "sweat." This is rather surprising since its pages are frequented by accounts of slavery, warfare, desert travel, construction, and all manner of physical exertion. The three instances, however, serve the purpose of emphasizing the fallen state of man through Adam, the holiness of God, and the appalling cost of rescue and redemption.

> **They shall have linen turbans on their heads,**
> **and linen undergarments around their waists.**
> **They shall not bind themselves**
> **with anything that causes sweat.**
> **(Ezekiel 44:18 ESV)**

---

[12] Genesis 3:15.

In this passage the prophet Ezekiel speaks of an especially holy temple, both perfect in architecture and in function. He describes in precise detail its construction and its sanctified rituals and worship before the one and only being of holiness, the LORD God, the Singular, Eternal, Preexisting, Uncreated Being.

In the presence of unsullied glory and goodness, priestly attention to purity is paramount. Sweat, the product and result of the as yet unredeemed first sin, has no place in the habitation of God. This temple, after all, bears the trademark of perfection only owned by its LandLORD. And from its domain only pure, Eden-like, waters are permitted to flow. Ezekiel 47:12 (NIV) "Fruit trees of all kinds will grow on both banks of the river. Their leaves will not wither, nor will their fruit fail. Every month they will bear, because the water from the sanctuary flows to them. Their fruit will serve for food and their leaves for healing."

> **Jesus knew that the Father**
> **had put all things under his power,**
> **and that he had come from God**
> **and was returning to God …**
> **After that, he poured water into a basin and**
> **began to wash his disciples' feet,**
> **with the towel that was wrapped around him.**
> **(John 13:3, 5 NIV)**

Jesus Christ, humanity's second Adam and last chance at peace with God, on a momentous Thursday night, entered his own garden of decision. There he would sweat as no Adam has ever sweat. There his yes to the Father began a succession of events that by Sunday would nullify Adam's no. But first …

On that night, He gathered his twelve disciples into an "upper room"[13] in Jerusalem. His sermon ministry had opened three years earlier with the lengthy but deliciously wordy "Sermon on the Mount." It began with,

---

[13] Luke 22:12.

"Blessed are the poor in spirit for theirs is the kingdom of heaven." His final sermon, equally lengthy and luscious,[14] opens not with words. Instead Jesus models the thoroughly compassionate, selfless humility he had called for in his Sermon on the Mount. On mortal knees, Jesus takes of the H_2O he, himself, spoke into existence, and washes and dries the dusty, smelly, road-weary feet of his disciples.

The same Ezekiel who five hundred years earlier spoke of a holy, sin-free temple prophesied this moment and those to come in the next three days. Ezekiel 36:25 (NLT): "Then I will sprinkle clean water on you, and you will be clean. Your filth will be washed away, and you will no longer worship idols."

When Jesus had spoken these words,
He went out with His disciples over the
Brook Kidron. (John 18:1 NKJV)

In less than twenty-four hours, Jesus, the creator and master of lakes and rivers, will cry out from the cross, "I thirst." As if in preface to that moment, the Bible records him crossing the Brook Kidron to the Garden of Gethsemane. Any human novelist would have him, marching to triumph, across a Euphrates, Nile, or even Jordan River. But the Brook Kidron? What is a brook but a pygmy creek hardly worth notation on a map? And the Kidron? Mostly a gulch devoid of even a drop of water most of the year. Still, over the Kidron he goes. "Blessed are the poor in spirit for theirs is the kingdom of God."

But the Bible story is not the fictional work of a Dickens, Tolstoy, or Hemingway. It is the very documentary of God's history with man. It is an account of redemption and salvation built upside-down. The LORD God presents his Son, Jesus Christ, as the sacrifice man is unable to pay—the perfect sinless gift laid down at the altar of reconciliation. Out of his

---

[14] John 13–16.

appalling and undeserved thirst flows the amazing and underserved grace that is our "living water."[15]

When Jesus had spoken these words,
He went out with His disciples over the Brook
Kidron ... (John 18:1 NKJV)

The Bible, though composed of sixty-six books, is a seamless work of revelation. It repeatedly peers to the future, recalls the past, and overlaps both in order to highlight and magnify its chief object—Jesus Christ. Here the "garden" recalls Adam's garden of failure and defeat. And here it peers forward to another garden, which Sunday will house an empty tomb. And here it peers distantly ahead to Ezekiel's restored garden of sinless joy.

And being in an agony he prayed more earnestly.
(Luke 22:44 ESV)

The sinless heaven-sent God-human, now voluntary resident of the cursed planet earth, is about to shed sweat of a most unique brand, "like great drops of blood."[16] We have no evidence that Adam and Eve nursed much, if any, anxiety in the face of temptation. They just plain found it tasty, beautiful, and profitable, and dove in headfirst. That's about how alienation from God usually works. We don't give much thought to it.

Not so, Jesus. He agonized over a temptation to "abort the mission." But he did not agonize alone. He took it to his father, the LORD God, in prayer. What he saw before him was a cup, not of living water, but of swamp-soaked death. His, and his only, was a vessel brimmed with the sin of everyone but himself. He alone must not only taste but drink fully of its filth. In that reality, he cries out a plea and a pledge.

Father, if you are willing,
please take this cup of suffering away from me.

---

[15] Jeremiah 17:13, Zechariah 14:8, John 4:4–29, John 7:37–39.
[16] Luke 22:44.

> **Yet I want your will to be done, not mine."**
> **And being in an agony**
> **he prayed more earnestly;**
> **and his sweat became like great drops of blood**
> **falling down to the ground. (Luke 22:44 ESV)**

Well it is that Jesus should sweat. The Bible writers record only two people in sweat: the first Adam and the Second Adam. The first sweats in condemnation for sin and rebellion, his own. The second sweats in condemnation for sin and rebellion, not his own, but that of the first Adam and of all mankind

Well it is that he should sweat. And well it is that he should sweat as no other human has. For he will suffer and die as no other human has. It is Thursday. His arrest, trial, and death await. This very night, he will be abandoned by his disciples. Three years he has trained, nurtured, and loved these men. Tonight, three times, as he prays, asking them to stay awake, they will drift off. Three times his trusted right-hand man, Peter, will deny knowledge of him.

Well it is that he should sweat. As Adam sweats drops into the dust to which he deserves to return, so Jesus sheds his into the ground, symbolic of the undeserved earth-bound vault into which he will soon be sealed. Well it is that the Savior, about to be flailed, punctured, and sliced, should shed sweat "like great drops of blood." The drops will soon be actual blood. And they will be profuse.

PART II

Desolation and Consolation

What Are People?

**When I look at the night sky and
see the work of your fingers—
the moon and the stars you set in place—
what are people that you should think about them,
mere mortals that you should care for them?
(Psalm 8:3–4 New Living Translation)**

The psalmist asserts as truth an assumption now increasingly dismissed among contemporaries. God cares for people. The poet has searched the vast heavens only to turn the telescope on himself. He discovers quantitative and qualitative insignificance. Finding himself microscopic in stature, intelligence, and capability, he can only respond in prideless poverty of spirit. "What are people…?" The skeptic interrupts, "People are water and chemicals packaged in chaos and destined for nothingness." The psalmist answers, "You didn't let me finish. 'What are people … that God should even think about them or care for them?'"

And in this hypothetical exchange lies the question that must be answered by all. Are humans yet the treasured consummation of the LORD God's once "very good" creation? Or are they merely quarts of water, molecules, and trace elements of earth packaged in chaos and destined for nothingness?

> **When I look at the night sky**
> **and see the work of your fingers—**
> **the moon and the stars you set in place—**
> **what are people that you should think about them,**
> **mere mortals that you should care for them?**
> **(Psalm 8:3–4 NLT)**

Are humans yet the treasured consummation of the LORD God's once "very good" creation? Or are they merely quarts of water, molecules, and trace elements of earth packaged in chaos and destined for nothingness? The case for the latter is asserted more and more frequently—perhaps never better than in the following:

> "You are water. I'm water
> We're all water in different containers
> That's why it's so easy to meet
> Someday we'll evaporate together."
> —Yoko Ono

The psalmist thinks diametrically otherwise and continues his song:

> **For You have made Him a little lower than the angels,**
> **And You have crowned Him with glory and honor.**
> **(Psalm 8:5 NKJV)**

"You have crowned him with glory and honor." One must wonder if the psalmist had read the first three chapters of Genesis. We can be assured he did. The very first psalm itself sets the standard for immersion into the Bible. "Blessed is the man," it proclaims, "whose delight is in the law of the LORD, and in his law he meditates day and night. (NKJV)

Last we heard, however, there was more than mere "trouble in paradise." It was closed for business, its gates shuttered and guarded, angelically forbidding occupancy. Adam and Eve were last seen on the run with only God-provided shirts on their previously bare backs. "And the LORD God made for Adam and for his wife garments of skins and clothed them." (Genesis 3:21 ESV)

The God as tailor and clothier passage above is critical because it dramatically notes the LORD God's personal and intentional care and concern for his flawed and rebellious, but infinitely redeemable, creation. And it will be the infinite one himself who will provide the ultimate and consummate redemption. The story is book-length. The finished volume is the Bible. Its pages are saturated with the imagery of the king of chemistry—H_2O— from deluges, storm-driven shipwrecks, to still and thirst-quenching water.

O LORD, OUR LORD,
HOW EXCELLENT IS YOUR NAME IN ALL THE EARTH.
You have made [man] to have dominion
over the works of Your hands;
You have put all things under his feet, All sheep
and oxen—Even the beasts of the field,
The birds of the air, And the fish of the sea
that pass through the paths of the seas.
O LORD, OUR LORD,
HOW EXCELLENT IS YOUR NAME IN ALL THE EARTH.
(Psalm 8:1, 6–9 NKJV)

Hundreds of years before Christ, when the eighth Psalm was written, a lot of water had flowed under the Biblical bridge—most of it turbulent. Here, however, the author reminds readers that man remains the sole custodian of the LORD God's domain. Land, sea, air, and of all that walk, swim, and soar thereon fall under human "dominion."

So as to preclude any sense of human superiority, however, the reader is reminded that the entire planet is the work of the LORD's hands, and it is the LORD who has delegated to man his lofty guardianship. The Beginning and the End, the Alpha and Omega, encloses the entire flow chart within a praiseful start and finish reminder, "O LORD, our LORD, how excellent is your name in all the earth."

Noah

**The LORD saw that the wickedness of man
was great in the earth,
and that every intention of the thoughts of his heart
was only evil continually.
(Genesis 6:5 ESV)**

Adam and Eve were endowed with much more than the shirts on their backs. The LORD gifted them with long life, many children, and a prolific family tree. Nomadic as well as city life, music and metal working were introduced through their descendants.[17]

Unfortunately, their proclivity to bad choice was passed to the kids. Two murders are reported, the first being that of their second son by his older brother. Jealousy and polygamous marital strife seem to have initiated the second.[18]

It got much worse. The LORD saw in human action only great wickedness and in all the intentions of human thought only continual evil. About five hundred times the Bible employs the word *wicked* and about five hundred times the word *evil*. Judgment invariably accompanies both. While the LORD is repeatedly said to be "slow to anger" and "abounding in steadfast love," his endurance has limits. As men, women, and even children in our times cry out for retribution in the face of depravity, so the LORD also can be stretched beyond the limits of his patience and His mercy.

**The LORD saw that the wickedness of man
was great in the earth,
and that every intention of the thoughts of his heart**

---

[17] Genesis 4 and 5.
[18] Genesis 4:1–8, 4:19–21.

> was only evil continually.
> The LORD was grieved that he had made man on
> the earth, and his heart was filled with pain.
> (Genesis 6:5–6 ESV)

Once again man's response to the LORD's benevolence is disdain and dismissal of his moral authority and very being. This time, however, his rebellion is thorough to the point of great wickedness and continual evil thoughts.

Moses, the writer of Genesis, phrases man's brazen challenge to the LORD with this couplet: "wickedness" and "evil." In absolute contrast, he characterizes the LORD's initial response in couplet form, as well: "grieved" and "pain." And to both man and the LORD, he places their motives and emotions into an essence of their being—the heart. Eight hundred times the Bible will employ this term as an entity of the *mind, will,* and *understanding.*

God's word will continually call men and women to a "heart after God." It will continually remind us that though God be aggrieved and pained to the uttermost, he is slow to anger, abounding in steadfast love and faithful to save and deliver.

> So the LORD said,
> "I will blot out man
> whom I have created from the face of the land,
> man and animals and creeping things
> and birds of the heavens,
> for I am sorry that I have made them."
> But Noah found favor in the eyes of the LORD.
> (Genesis 6:7–8 ESV)

"So" and "but."

"So the LORD said, 'I will blot out man ...'" The Bible often begins a sentence with "so" or "therefore," indicating that the previously disclosed information foreshadows a result that is about to be disclosed. In this case, the LORD has been described as grieved to the fullness of pain by wickedness and evil. The result is regret so immense that he will "blot out" from the land and sky all that he has created.

"But" and "however." The Bible frequently tags "so" with "but" or "however," indicating the disclosed situation and reality is about to be amended in some manner. In this case, though man's sin is so grievous as to be divinely unbearable, the LORD will extend undeserved mercy. Moderns have put that concept to music and call it "Amazing Grace,"[19] a staple of the LORD's merciful handling of his willful band of rebels—man.

"But Noah found favor in the eyes of the LORD."

> **So the LORD said,**
> **"I will blot out man whom I have created**
> **from the face of the land,**
> **man and animals and creeping things**
> **and birds of the heavens,**
> **for I am sorry that I have made them."**
> **But Noah found favor in the eyes of the LORD.**
> **(Genesis 6:7–8 ESV)**

The entirety of God's earthly creation, save two entities, now faces destruction soon to be described in the form of a massive flood. Man, represented by Noah, his wife, his sons, and their wives,[20] along with the inhabitants of the water and sky, appear at this point to possess the only exemptions. Why are they spared? Unmerited amazing grace in action. Even Noah, while apparently exemplary among his pre-flood peers, falls far short of perfection. He will become the first recorded victim of the curse of the "bottle." Unexpectedly, after being saved from destruction, we find him inebriated to unconsciousness.[21] Ensuing events lead to the first post-deluge family dysfunction.

---

[19] "Amazing Grace" hymn by John Newton.
[20] Genesis 7:7.
[21] Genesis 9:29–27.

Land and a host of sky creatures, innocent victims of Adam's curse and his descendants' indiscretions, face the death sentence; while water bound animals will be spared. As will be seen throughout scripture, water comes to man and nature as an object lesson both in God's turbulent righteous judgment and his gently flowing mercy.

> **The earth was depraved**
> **and putrid in God's sight and**
> **the land was filled with violence,**
> **(desecration, infringement, outrage,**
> **assault and lust for power).**
> **And God looked upon the world and saw how**
> **degenerate, debased and vicious it was;**
> **for all humanity had corrupted their way upon**
> **the earth and lost their true direction.**
> **(Genesis 6:11–12 Amplified Bible)**

The Amplified Bible attempts to grasp and transmit into English the breadth and depth of the original language. Here it is Hebrew. And here the breadth and depth of human debauchery and rebellion is depicted as beyond comprehension and beyond restoration.

Power had corrupted man. He lusted after it to the uttermost. He, who had been blessed with dominion over earth, now deemed his divine donor irrelevant. Power had corrupted him. The pitiful illusion of absolute power had now corrupted him absolutely.

All humanity had lost its "true direction." Only divinity could reset and restore the madly spinning, out of control, compass that had once pointed all human beings to himself.

> **Noah was a righteous man,**
> **blameless among the people of his time,**
> **and he walked with God. (Genesis 6:9 NIV)**

A repeated biblical theme, from Noah through the final biblical book of Revelation, is that of the "remnant." An entire world seems to have eagerly sped down the boulevard of madness bound for the freeway of destruction. Like pedestrians dodging the traffic mayhem, a few God fearers and God lovers dangerously trek the perilously narrow path of righteousness. Only divine intervention protects them on their hazardous way.

Like Noah, the biblical remnant will invariably fall far short of full righteousness, of blamelessness. They may stumble on the path, veer to the curb, or even take an occasional hit.

Their worth is not reckoned by the yardstick of flawless character or morality but by the tape of a heart set in pursuit of God's own heart.

> **And God said to Noah,**
> **"I have determined to make an end of all flesh,**
> **For the earth is filled with violence through them.**
> **Behold, I will destroy them with the earth.**
> **Make yourself an ark."**
> **(Genesis 6:13–14 ESV)**

God now speaks directly to Noah. His ruminations on the state of his terribly disunified union have resulted in a momentous decision. The earth, as known to that point, has to go.

Before Noah can ask, "What about me and the wife and the kids?" God preempts the question.

"Make an ark." A command is issued in three words soon to be expanded to the blueprint for the world's first shipbuilding enterprise. Noah is to construct a boat of about 450 feet in length, 75 feet in width and 45 feet in height.

On this ship he is to house and feed through a forty-day flood his family and himself as well as one male and one female of all fleshly species—in the cases of "clean" animals and birds seven of a kind.[22]

Why the LORD God did not carry out his mission of judgment through earthquake, wind, or fire is not disclosed. However, we do find that water for the first of many, many occasions will demonstrate the power of God's sovereignty—often through disruption and devastation. It will also and even more often demonstrate his compassion and mercy shown through deliverance and consolation. The ark will role model God's provision of a buoyant agent of redemption in the face of overwhelming darkness and sin.

> **For behold,**
> **I will bring a flood of waters upon the earth**
> **to destroy all flesh**
> **in which is the breath of life under heaven.**
> **Everything that is on the earth shall die.**
> **But I will establish my covenant with you,**
> **and you shall come into the ark,**
> **you, your sons, your wife, and your sons' wives**
> **with you. (Genesis 6:17–18 ESV)**

For the first time, the LORD discloses the format of judgment. It will be water. It will be sufficient "to destroy all flesh in which is the breath of life under heaven." It will be sufficient to kill everything on earth. Enter the large print disclaimer—"but." A special exemption is granted, as promised, to the Noah clan. No sooner is "flood" added to the Bible vocabulary list than it is joined by "covenant." "Covenant" will by far be employed more numerously through the Bible. In this word lies a progressive revelation of God's care and preservation of humanity and of the people he loves. And it all begins with an ark.

> **And Noah and his sons and his wife**
> **and his sons' wives with him**

---

[22] Genesis 6:19–7:4.

> went into the ark to escape the waters of the flood.
> Of clean animals, and of animals that are not clean,
> and of birds, and of everything that creeps on the ground,
> two and two, male and female,
> went into the ark with Noah,
> as God had commanded Noah.
> And after seven days the waters of the flood
> came upon the earth. (Genesis 7:7–10 ESV)

With the ark built and the cargo loaded, all is in readiness. Then, almost as if all creation is granted one last reminiscence of the "good" and "very good" old days of creation, judgment is delayed a week.

Eight humans, aboard history's first cruise ship, are registered with the creatures of the world's first and finest zoo and await their stormy departure. The dry land on which the ship sits is about to become the world's first, though short-lived, port. Voyage duration: unknown. Destination: unknown.

Thousands of years ahead of the Titanic, the HMS *Ark* is truly the "unsinkable ship." Who is its Designer, Construction Foreman, Captain, Helmsman, and Cruise Director rolled into one? He is none other than the Singular, Eternal, Preexisting, Uncreated Being who created all that is from that which was not. And he is intent on preserving his investment.

> The flood continued forty days on the earth.
> The waters increased and bore up the ark,
> and it rose high above the earth.
> And all flesh died that moved on the earth,
> birds, livestock, beasts,
> all swarming creatures that swarm on the earth,
> and all mankind.
> Only Noah was left
> and those who were with him in the ark.
> And the waters prevailed on the earth 150 days.
> (Genesis 7:17, 21, 23–24 ESV)

In six days the LORD God had created the heavens and the earth. Now in righteous judgment on unrestrained sin and rejection, he storms the bastions of his creation with forty days of flood and with another 110 days of standing water. Every living thing in the storm's wake lies deceased below its high tide. Above, the rescued survivors breathe deeply of fresh, restorative postflood air. God's investment is preserved.

> **In the second month,**
> **on the twenty-seventh day of the month,**
> **the earth had dried out.**
> **Then God said to Noah,**
> **"Go out from the ark, you and your wife,**
> **and your sons and your sons' wives with you.**
> **Bring out with you every living thing**
> **that is with you of all flesh—**
> **birds and animals and every creeping thing that creeps on the earth—**
> **that they may swarm on the earth,**
> **and be fruitful and multiply on the earth."**
> **(Genesis 8:14–17 ESV)**

After about a year aboard ship, the population is ordered to their feet and paws. "Go out from the ark." The rescue is complete. Lower the gangplank. I lead them out. If only a video had been taken. Imagine the wobbly giraffe sea legs.

There is serious business ahead, however. Restoration. The bipeds, quadrupeds, and centipedes are all commanded to "be fruitful and multiply." The mandate has been heard before. It had been issued in better times. God's very first conversation was with his sky and sea animals. "Be fruitful and multiply." It was the fifth day of creation and was said to be "good." The next was pronounced "very good," and on that day he authorized Adam to not only "be fruitful and multiply" but to "subdue" the earth and have "dominion" over it.

One 360-degree survey of the battered land and rescinding water demonstrates clearly that the generous LandLORD -tenant agreement has been forever altered. A last affectionate gaze at the decommissioned ship, nonetheless, verifies the LandLORD's continued interest in a relationship. He had assured a buoyant protection through the storm. His promise has been fulfilled.

> **Every beast, every creeping thing, and every bird,**
> **everything that moves on the earth,**
> **went out by families from the ark.**
> **Then Noah built an altar to the LORD**
> **and took some of every clean animal**
> **and some of every clean bird**
> **and offered burnt offerings on the altar.**
> **(Genesis 8:19–20 ESV)**

The disembarking completed, Noah's first act is to honor and worship the LORD of his deliverance. The LORD had commanded seven of every clean animal to be taken aboard the ark.

Safe ashore Noah responding, not to a mandate to sacrifice but to the gratitude of his own heart, gleans the singletons from the remaining three pairs and burns them in tribute to the master of land, sea, and air. The LORD's amazing grace is reciprocated in the sweet aroma of Noah's amazed gratitude.

> **And when the LORD smelled the pleasing aroma,**
> **the LORD said in his heart,**
> **"I will never again curse the ground because of man,**
> **for the intention of man's heart is evil from his youth.**
> **Neither will I ever again strike down**
> **every living creature as I have done.**
> **While the earth remains,**
> **seedtime and harvest, cold and heat,**
> **summer and winter, day and night, shall not**
> **cease." (Genesis 8:21–22 ESV)**

The divine name, LORD, reenters the narrative at the altar of gratitude. It has been 100 percent absent in the flood narrative from the closing of the ark's doors to Noah's firing up of the altar of praise. Why? The "LORD" connotes an unknowable, unshared, out of time and place eternal sovereign, translating something close to "I Am that I Am." How fitting a title for the creator of all things and the destroyer of so much.

The book of Genesis screams out, "divinely inspired."

Not the wildest imagination of religion, myth, or fable has ever created the likes of an I Am that I Am. Had such a man-made deity been concocted, any accompanying flood story would look entirely different. Its god of gods would soar in vengeful, derisive delight over its gasping, flailing, drowning, creation. An I Am who not only rescues but reinstates the very species who would dethrone him would have to have a "heart." See above.

> And when the LORD smelled the pleasing aroma,
> the LORD said in his heart,
> "I will never again curse the ground because of man,
> for the intention of man's heart is evil from his youth.
> Neither will I ever again strike down
> every living creature as I have done.
> While the earth remains,
> seedtime and harvest, cold and heat,
> summer and winter, day and night, shall not
> cease." (Genesis 8:21–22 ESV)

Two truths about "heart" were disclosed before the flood: (1) man's heart: "Every imagination of the thoughts of his heart was only evil continually." (2) The LORD's heart: "It grieved him at his heart."[23] Sin, we find, is so ugly and reprehensible to him that it must be purged at horrific cost.

The cost has been paid. And maybe Charles Dickens's opening to *Tale of Two Cities* captures the moment. "It was the best of times. It was the worst of

---

[23] Genesis 6:5.

times." Amid the devastation of a violent divine wrath, a momentarily better human heart pulses in devotion, and the LORD is pleased. Two hearts, one of mortal flesh and the other of eternal spirit, beat, ever so briefly, as one.

> **And when the LORD smelled the pleasing aroma,**
> **the LORD said in his heart,**
> **"I will never again curse the ground because of man,**
> **for the intention of man's heart is evil from his youth.**
> **Neither will I ever again strike down**
> **every living creature as I have done.**
> **While the earth remains,**
> **seedtime and harvest,**
> **cold and heat,**
> **summer and winter, day and night, shall not**
> **cease." (Genesis 8:21–22 ESV)**

Things are looking up. The LORD promises he will never again "strike down every living creature as I have done." Seasons will come. They will go. Days will die in darkness and be reborn in light. This is one big sweet-scented heart-to-heart bonfire. Reunited at last!

Not exactly. As usual, in scripture, observe context. No secrets, even this early in the "reset" game. "I will never again curse the ground because of man, for the intention of man's heart is evil from his youth." As it happens, the LORD's heartfelt kindness emerges not because of a projected goodness in man's heart but *in spite the intentions of his heart remaining evil even from his youth.*

It appears the intention of neither heart is going to change. When you are the "I am," it can't. When you are natural man, it doesn't and won't.

The Rainbow Covenant

> **Then God said to Noah and to his sons with him,**
> **I will establish my covenant with you;**
> **Neither shall all flesh be cut off any more**

> **By the waters of a flood;**
> **Neither shall there anymore**
> **Be a flood to destroy the earth.**
> **(Genesis 9:8, 11 ESV)**

The LORD has completed his heart-to-heart conference with himself. He now announces to Noah and his sons the establishment of a "covenant."[24] He vows that never again will all flesh be cut off by a flood, nor will a deluge destroy the earth. The promise is declared in spite of his knowledge that the heart of his prize creation will remain intransigent from "his youth." Noah had been summoned into the ark with a covenant guaranteeing protection and survival to his family and animal passengers.[25] Having now delivered on the flood insurance, God extends the warranty to all generations to follow.

> **Then God said,**
> **"I am giving you a sign of my covenant with you**
> **And with all living creatures,**
> **For all generations to come.**
> **I have placed my rainbow in the clouds.**
> **It is the sign of my covenant with you**
> **and with all the earth." (Genesis 9:12–13 NLT)**

"I am giving you ..." Whenever we see a rainbow, we observe the sign of an ancient treaty between God and man—a unilateral treaty. The belligerent rebels have been swept from the field. Only a single merchant vessel with its sea-weary crew of eight has survived. The sailors breathe another day courtesy of wartime diplomatic immunity provided by God.

Captain Noah offers a sacrificial fire of acknowledged debt and sincere appreciation. It is a temporary accord between man and God. Peace cannot be sustained, for the "intention of man's heart is evil from his youth." It

---

[24] "Covenant" is a word that Biblically conveys a contractual sense of commitment and unity of purpose. Normally it is partnered with the "LORD" indicating a special relationship between the "I am" and his people. Here, in context of a new start for earth, it pairs with "God" (Eloheim), the majestic creator of the heavens and the earth.
[25] Genesis 6:18.

will not be long before God will again have ample reason to punish his creation. And why not this time make a true end to it, completely destroying humanity?

Instead, God places where all can see it a promise in the sky recurring as long as there are rain and clouds. It will be an ironclad guarantee that he will never again destroy earth by flood. His oath is so strong as to invoke the word "covenant" seven times in a clear reminder of the seventh day of restful peace that followed six days of creation.[26]

> When I see the rainbow in the clouds,
> I will remember the eternal covenant
> between God and every living creature on earth."
> Then God said to Noah,
> "Yes, this rainbow is the sign of the covenant
> I am confirming with all the creatures on earth."
> (Genesis 9:16–17 NLT)

So what kind of treaty is this? A strange unilateral one containing no oppressive penalties, humiliation, or loss of sovereignty. No mention is even made of moral obligation on the part of the defeated toward the victor, just more divine initiation of amazing grace. God's self-control in the face of belligerence is to extend to all humans yet to live—those who will seek him, those who will turn their backs on him, and those indifferent.

Perhaps in proof that the "intention of man's heart is evil from his youth," one rather large contemporary segment of Noah's current descendants associates rainbows only with the illusionary promise of gold at its end.

The unilateral rainbow covenant imposes just one condition. And irony of ironies—it is not upon the helpless defeated combatants but on the triumphant all-powerful victor. "Remember." "When I [God] see the rainbow in the clouds, I will remember the eternal covenant between God and every living creature on earth."

---

[26] Genesis 9:9–17.

Ezekiel's Rainbow

In the thirtieth year, in the fourth month on the fifth day,
while I was among the exiles by the Kebar River,
the heavens were opened and I saw visions of God
All around him was a glowing halo, like a rainbow
shining in the clouds on a rainy day. This is what
the glory of the LORD looked like to me.
When I saw it, I fell face down on the ground,
and I heard someone's voice speaking to me.
(Ezekiel 1:1, 28 NIV)

It is likely that millions of rainbows have been viewed by the billions of earth's inhabitants. The Bible, post-Noah, accounts for only three. The prophet Ezekiel considers his sighting so noteworthy as to cite the precise day.[27] He and his fellow Israelites are a long way from home, war exiles in the foreign land of Babylonia. It is a land of predictable abundance sustained by not one but two of the world's greatest rivers—the Tigris and Euphrates. Yet like the land of the Nile, these rivers, this land, and its capital, Babylon, endure throughout the Bible as symbols of man's idolatry and immorality and of the LORD God's judgment and deliverance.

It is along Babylonia's Kebar River[28] that Israelite captive Ezekiel receives a vision of the LORD God. His appearance defies any description short of an astonishing entity enclosed in a "glowing halo, like a rainbow shining in the clouds on a rainy day."

Says Ezekiel,
"This is what the glory of the LORD looked like to me."

---

[27] Moses, recording the Genesis rainbow, also notes the precise day of the year in which the first rainbow appeared. Genesis 8:13–14.

[28] The Chebar (alternate spellings—Kebar, Habar, Chebaras) is associated with the Euphrates and perhaps was a canal connecting the Tigris and the Euphrates.

The Revelation Rainbow

**And instantly I was in the Spirit,
and I saw a throne in heaven and someone sitting on it.
The one sitting on the throne was as brilliant as
gemstones—like jasper and carnelian.
And the glow of an emerald circled his throne
like a rainbow. (Revelation 4:2–3 NLT)**

When lost for words to describe a vision of the Singular, Eternal, Preexisting, and Uncreated being, try "rainbow." Jesus Christ's disciple, John, spent three years with God in the flesh as his disciple. Now, "in the Spirit," he views him resurrected and ascended into heaven, victorious over death and Satan.

Jesus Christ reigns, as he always has, but even more resplendent, as the everlasting God Man. Like Ezekiel, hundreds of years earlier, John has no experience in the majestic indescribable things of heaven. How does one express the inexpressible? Desperate for words, he reaches into his reservoir of human awe and delight. He extracts the grandeur that most merges the beauty and promise of the heavens with the fresh, fragrant, dripping glory of earth after a storm.

**The one sitting on the throne was as brilliant as
gemstones—like jasper and carnelian.
And the glow of an emerald
circled his throne like a rainbow.
Revelation 4:3**

**Then I saw another mighty angel
coming down from heaven,
surrounded by a cloud, with a rainbow over His head.
His face shone like the sun, and
his feet were like pillars of fire.
(Revelation 10:1 NLT)**

John for the second and last time ascribes the beauty, majesty, and promise of the rainbow to Jesus Christ. He has seen many angels. None approach the glory of this one. With a cloud surrounding him and feet like pillars of fire, He can only be the eternal LORD (I AM).[29] In the time of Moses, the LORD originated and orchestrated the escape of his people, the Israelites, from slavery in Egypt. He revealed himself and his will in those days in a cloud by day and a pillar of fire by night. In this predictable and promising fashion, the LORD provided certainty and security in the midst of uncertain and insecure of times.

Now in an "end-times" reference, the I Am, the beginning and the end, the Alpha and Omega of the ancient Israelites, reveals himself in a cloud, pillars of fire, and with a rainbow above his head. It is not ancient Egypt and the Nile from which His people ultimately need deliverance. It is from the dirty waters of a polluted Euphrates and a sin-ridden Babylon that they must be finally and eternally rescued.

The Bible-length promise of heavenly deliverance and safety for God's people along with judgment upon his enemies is at hand. The last rainbow, backlit by a "face that shone like the sun," prefaces redemption delivered.

Abraham

Now the LORD had said to Abram:
"Get out of your country, From your family
And from your father's house,
to a land that I will show you."
(Genesis 12:1 NKJV)

The "country" from which Abram was to exit was none other than the splendid fertile cradle of civilization called Mesopotamia—the land between the rivers. This was Abram's second move and one that would shape the future course of history. The LORD, unilaterally, in yet another merciful rescue, is calling a lone man out of the despair and dead end of

---

[29] John 8:58.

idolatry. And to Abram's descendants (the Hebrews), and through Jesus Christ, he would issue the same call.

Abram[30] was born in Ur near deltas of the mighty Euphrates and Tigris rivers. His father, Terah, moved the family a great distance to dwell at Haran along a tributary of the Euphrates.

The LORD called Abram away from Haran, from everything that a natural heart would hold dear—the predictability and security of well-watered land, the commercial glitz, glamour, and "cool" of trade centers such as Ur and Haran, and the allure of their seductive gods. In exchange, Abram was summoned by the Singular, Eternal, Preexisting, and Uncreated Being to the yet to be revealed "land that I will show you."

> **"I will make you a great nation;**
> **I will bless you and make your name great;**
> **And you shall be a blessing.**
> **I will bless those who bless you,**
> **And I will curse him who curses you;**
> **And in you all the families of the earth shall**
> **be blessed." (Genesis 12:2–3 NKJV)**

It is rather typical of the LORD that in every admonition in which man is called to "leave" is coupled a lucrative blessing for him to "enter".

Immediately after commanding Abram to abandon Mesopotamia and its allures, he promises (covenants) to construct from this single man a "great nation" and a "great name." Abram will be blessed while his detractors will be cursed.

It is a one-way covenant. Everything is active on the LORD God's part and passive on Abrams's and his descendants'. They *will* become a great nation

---

[30] The LORD later changed his name to Abraham. Genesis 17:5 ESV) No longer shall your name be called Abram, but your name shall be Abraham, for I have made you the father of a multitude of nations.

and be blessed; their name *will* be great, and they *will* be a blessing; those who bless them *will* be blessed, and those who curse them *will* be cursed. And in spite of their foot-dragging, obstinacy, and defiance, all the families of the earth *shall* be blessed.

It turns out there will be, in Abram's rather dysfunctional historic family, a near death wish *not* to be a blessing to anyone. "You could look it up."[31]

> **Then He [the LORD] brought him outside and said,**
> **"Look now toward heaven, and count the stars**
> **If you are able to number them."**
> **And He said to him, "So shall your descendants be."**
> **And he believed in the LORD, and**
> **He accounted it to him for righteousness.**
> **Then He said to him, "I am the LORD,**
> **who brought you out of Ur of the Chaldeans,**
> **to give you this land to inherit it."**
> **(Genesis 15:5–7 NKJV)**

This renewal of the covenant promise comes in the midst of more than reasonable doubt on the part of Abram. He and his wife, Sarah, have reached ages far beyond child-bearing. Sarah hasn't delivered, and as far as Abram is concerned, neither has the LORD. In dramatic response, the LORD sends out Abram to survey the night skies in search of the number of the stars. So also shall his descendants be calculated.

Further reading tells us that the LORD, as always, has the last laugh. The old-timers will indeed have a son to inherit Abram's promise and pass it on. His name, Isaac, in Hebrew, translates to "laughter," in playful reminder of the skeptical mirth Mom and Dad had expressed at the very thought of old-age maternity.

> **Then He [the LORD] brought him outside and said,**
> **"Look now toward heaven, and count the stars**
> **if you are able to number them."**

---

[31] From James Thurber and many others.

And He said to him, "So shall your descendants be."
And he believed in the LORD, and
He accounted it to him for righteousness.
Then He said to him, "I am the LORD,
who brought you out of Ur of the Chaldeans,
to give you this land to inherit it."
(Genesis 15:5–7 NKJV)

The don't-miss-it passage here is, "He [Abram] believed in the LORD and he [The LORD] "accounted it to him for righteousness." Neither Abram nor any of his descendants would or could merit or earn righteousness or be made righteous in the sight of the LORD. Not by their own actions, even the best intentioned and most fruitful of them, could they blot out their sinful nature, intents, and deeds. It is by faith, through amazing grace, generated by the LORD that Abram believed. And it is by faith, through amazing grace, that every Abram to come will believe. Paul, the prolific New Testament writer, puts it as follows:

Abraham was, humanly speaking, the founder of the Jewish nation. What did he discover about being made right with God? If his good deeds had made him acceptable to God, he would have had something to boast about. But that was not God's way. For the scriptures tell us, "Abraham believed God, and God counted him as righteous because of his faith." (Romans 4:1–3 NLT)

Then He [the LORD] brought him outside and said,
"Look now toward heaven, and
count the stars if you are able to number them."
And He said to him, "So shall your descendants be."
And he believed in the LORD, and
He accounted it to him for righteousness.
Then He said to him, "I am the LORD,
who brought you out of Ur of the Chaldeans,
to give you this land to inherit it."
(Genesis 15:5–7 NKJV)

And the LORD's clincher on the whole matter? It is ultimately about him, not Abram, his descendants or any of their detractors. The Singular, Eternal, Preexisting and Uncreated Being, I AM, has called you out of the idolatrous darkness of "Ur of the Chaldeans" to give you this land to inherit it.

What sense could that make to the graying, wrinkling, creaking Abraham when told he will be father to multitudes? What sense could it make to trade the known for the unknown? Why give up the lucrative waters and fertile soils of the Tigris and Euphrates for an unseen far away "land?" Foolishness! Scripture responds to that exclamation point with one of its own. From the New King James Version: "The foolishness of God is wiser than men, and the weakness of God is stronger than men."[32]

> **Now there was a famine in the land,**
> **and Abram went down to Egypt to dwell there,**
> **for the famine was severe in the land.**
> **(Genesis 12:10 NKJV)**

Abram, along with his wife and nephew, Lot, and a considerable entourage of servants and livestock, proceeded as ordered into the special land that the LORD had promised. Its major waterways still exist, but by any reasonable world standard none qualify as all-star. The Biblically storied river, the Jordan, meanders little more than two hundred miles, flowing through the Sea of Galilee[33] and spilling its mouth into the very dead Dead Sea, a thoroughly salted and mineralized body of water at the lowest elevation on earth.[34]

The Bible does not record faithful Abram's initial impressions of this "inheritance" of his. It merely tells us that the land was afflicted by "severe famine," surely goaded to fullness by its close companion, "drought."

---

[32] 1 Corinthians 1:25.

[33] About eight by five miles, it is historically known also as Lake or Sea of Tiberias, of Kinneret, of Gennesaret.

[34] Thirty-five by eleven miles in size, thirteen hundred feet below sea level, with depth reaching twenty-three hundred feet below sea level.

Apparently with approval of the LORD, who provides no rebuke, Abram immigrates into the domain of splendid watery provision, Egypt.

Abram's grandson, Jacob, and his twelve boys will also venture famine driven, into the land along the Nile and live to tell the tale. In most other cases, Egypt and its river stand as symbols of insecurity, unfaithfulness, false hope, and despair.

> **And Lot lifted his eyes and saw all the plain of Jordan,**
> **that it was well watered everywhere**
> **(before the LORD destroyed Sodom and Gomorrah)**
> **like the garden of the LORD,**
> **like the land of Egypt as you go toward Zoar.**
> **Then Lot chose for himself all the plain of Jordan,**
> **and Lot journeyed east. (Genesis 13:10–11 NKJV)**

Abram and his nephew, Lot, returned from Egypt in safety and mutual prosperity. In fact, their flocks were so great that strife developed between herdsmen of Abram's flocks and those of Lot's. As may be suspected, water was again the challenge at hand. In a conflict resolution for the ages, Abram offers to Lot whatever land he wishes to claim, including the plain of the Jordan River, which was well watered everywhere.

This is the first of the Bible's nearly two hundred mentions of the Jordan. They are usually in context of God's deliverance into safety. Here the river valley is compared to the Garden of Eden and to the land of the Nile.

It was as futile for Lot to resist this land likened to Paradise as it was for his ancestors, Adam and Eve, to refuse the fruit of the tree of the knowledge of good and evil. He lifted his eyes, and they got the best of him. A later poor choice of Lot to move to the city of Sodom nearly cost him his life as the LORD rained down fire and brimstone, destroying the wicked inhabitants of Sodom and her sister in sin, Gomorrah.[35]

---

[35] See the remainder of Genesis 13 and Genesis 14 for the full account of Abraham, Lot, and Sodom and Gomorrah.

> Now the men of Sodom were wicked,
> great sinners against the LORD.
> The LORD said to Abram,
> after Lot had separated from him,
> "Lift up your eyes and look from the place where you are,
> northward and southward and eastward and westward,
> for all the land that you see I will give to you and to
> your offspring forever." (Genesis 13:13–15 ESV)

Lot, out of his own lustful will, "lifted his eyes" and chose the world's treasures at the expense of his uncle. He opted for the beautiful watered Jordan Valley. Then, harkening to worldly voices luring him to the door of sin and debauchery, he pitched his tent all the way to Sodom.

Abram's eyes were lifted, not on his own accord or self-will, but at the command of the LORD. North, south, east, and west he spun. Three hundred and sixty degrees—and all Abram could see was more "promised" land. All he could hear was the LORD's covenant repeated, "I will give to you and to your offspring forever."

Abram had held his eyes and ears in check awaiting a better image and a better voice. God rewarded his patient faith, not with earth's certain uncertainty but with heaven's blessed assurance.

> But Abram said to Sara,
> "Behold, your servant is in your power;
> To her as you please."
> Then Sara dealt harshly with her, and she fled from her.
> The angel of the LORD found her
> By a spring of water in the wilderness,
> the spring on the way to Shur.
> (Genesis 16:6–7 ESV)

The years dragged on, as did the accumulated birthdays of Abram and his wife, Sarai.[36] Sarai, desperate for an heir and long past child-bearing age, arranged a tryst between her husband and her Egyptian servant, Hagar.

The Holy Land soap opera commenced predictably. Hagar indeed found herself pregnant. Sarai perceived contempt from her maid servant, who now literally carried all the descendancy cards. Sarai, quickly having enough of inferiority, passed her complaints to the expectant papa. Papa, harboring no desire to play the referee, told Sarai to do as she wished. What she wished was to make Hagar's life miserable.

Hagar fled from her. The sordid earthy "soap" now took a decidedly heavenly twist. She made her way to a "spring," a bubbling, ever reliable source of pure restorative water. Here she received more than water. She encountered a one-of-a-kind being, the angel of the LORD.

> **The angel of the LORD said to her [Hagar],**
> **"Return to your mistress and submit to her."**
> **The angel of the LORD also said to her,**
> **"I will surely multiply your offspring**
> **So that they cannot be numbered for multitude."**
> **(Genesis 16:9–10 ESV)**

The last time the Bible spoke of angels was when the LORD barred the gates of Eden on the heels of the evicted Adam and Eve, leaving as guards a class of angels called cherubim. Not all angels, however, close doors, as Hagar is privileged to discover.

"Angel" is defined as "messenger," and angels appear throughout the Bible bearing both good news and bad. In the New Testament, angels often preface their message with, "Fear not." Though that greeting is not delivered at the spring, the message is exactly that. First bad news—head back to Sarai and submit. Then the good news— "I will surely multiply your offspring so that they cannot be numbered for multitude."

---

[36] The LORD later changed her name to Sarah, likely meaning "princess."

No angel is ordinary. An angel is very much a spiritual extraterrestrial of great magnitude. This angel is extraordinary to the infinite degree. Any angel could bear the disturbing message to "return to your mistress and submit to her." Only the LORD himself in angelic appearance could guarantee that he will "surely" multiply your offspring so that they cannot be numbered for multitude.

> **And the angel of the LORD said to her,**
> **"Behold, you are pregnant and shall bear a son.**
> **You shall call his name Ishmael,**
> **because the LORD has listened to your affliction.**
> **So she called the name of the LORD who spoke to her,**
> **"You are a God of seeing," for she said,**
> **"Truly here I have seen him who looks after me."**
> **(Genesis 16:11, 13 ESV)**

Hagar did not lack for affliction. The illicit baby-making was not her idea. Sarai, in a mind-set of faithlessness, and Abram, in abdication of his vaunted faith in the LORD's unconditional covenant, bound her to a night of adultery. Finding herself pregnant, she flaunted disdain for Sarai, opening herself to "harsh" treatment. One can imagine the sounds of "affliction" heard in Abraham's tent-dotted compound. The grapevine surely was alive with the dripping fruit of delicious gossip. Only the LORD, however, heard (and continues to hear) all things. He so noted Hagar's sorrow that he selected a name for the boy, "Ishmael—God hears."

In awe and amazed gratitude, she responded accordingly. Hagar paired the LORD's wondrous hearing with his compassionate sight. Hagar, the rejected, forlorn Egyptian, became the first person to assign an attribute to the I AM: "You are a God of seeing," for she said, "Truly here I have seen him who looks after me."

> **So Abraham rose early in the morning**
> **and took bread and a skin of water and gave it to Hagar,**
> **putting it on her shoulder,**
> **along with the child, and sent her away.**

> **And she departed and**
> **wandered in the wilderness of Beersheba.**
> **When the water in the skin was gone,**
> **she put the child under one of the bushes.**
> **(Genesis 21:14–15 ESV)**

At age ninety-nine, old man Abraham is once again guaranteed by the LORD that he will be the father of a great nation.[37] Not daunted by Sarai's geriatrics, the LORD delivers on his promise, and she just plain delivers. The bouncing baby Isaac arrives on the scene born to a dad of one hundred and a mom of ninety. Abram has been renamed as Abraham (the father of nations) and Sarai as Sarah (princess). What could be better? Well, there remains that problem of the other woman, the other boy, and the other covenant promise of nationhood.

Enter older brother Ishmael, now in his teens, who sets the already strained household into turmoil when he laughs at his little brother Isaac (meaning "laughter") struggling through the trials of weaning. Sarah, the biblical originator of laughter therapy, finds no humor in the situation and sets in motion the expulsion of Hagar and Ishmael. Abraham reluctantly sends them on their way with a prisoner's pittance—bread and water. Some inheritance. Some nation.

> **Then she [Hagar] went and**
> **sat down opposite him [Ishmael] a good way off,**
> **about the distance of a bowshot, for she said,**
> **"Let me not look on the death of the child."**
> **And as she sat opposite him,**
> **she lifted up her voice and wept.**
> **And God heard the voice of the boy,**
> **and the angel of God called to Hagar from heaven**
> **and said to her, "What troubles you, Hagar?**
> **Fear not, for God has heard**
> **the voice of the boy where he is.**

---

[37] Genesis 17.

> Up! Lift up the boy, and hold him fast with your hand,
> for I will make him into a great nation."
> Then God opened her eyes, and she saw a well of water.
> And she went and filled the skin with water
> and gave the boy a drink.
> (Genesis 21:17–19 ESV)

Ask any wilderness hiker how far a shoulder-load of water goes. Hagar, empty of life's fundamental staple, abandons Ishmael under the shade of a bush, puts distance between her and the doomed boy, and breaks into a voice muffled in the agony of wailing. This is the first record of weeping or crying in the Bible. The angel of God hears. He hears not only her voice but the voice of Ishmael. He is still as Hagar once said, "the God who sees." He is still the God who hears the voices of the outcast and oppressed. And the God who remembers his covenant promises.

Ishmael, will yet be the father of peoples who will inhabit the Middle East. Such bold promises, however, are fulfilled one day at a time. And now, in living evidence that there will be a tomorrow, Hagar's salted, watered eyes are opened to see a miraculous well of life giving fresh water.

Isaac and Jacob

> "But before I had finished speaking in my heart,
> there was Rebekah, coming out
> with her pitcher on her shoulder;
> and she went down to the well and drew water.
> And I said to her, 'Please let me drink.'
> "And she made haste and
> let her pitcher down from her shoulder, and said,
> 'Drink, and I will give your camels a drink also.'
> So I drank, and she gave the camels a drink
> also." (Genesis 24:45–46 NKJV)

Abraham was anxious that his covenant son Isaac not marry a woman from the idolatrous Canaanites among whom they lived. He sent a trusted servant back to his old homeland in Mesopotamia to find a wife in the land of his brother, Nahor. The servant arrived, bound by oath to get it right for Abraham and Isaac. He concocted in his mind a precise dialog that must come to pass between him and the "right girl." There it is above. He would ask in those words for a drink, and she would respond in exactly the premeditated phrase scripted.

Having perfectly fulfilled at the well his mandate, the servant returned to Abraham and Isaac with the blushing bride.

> **And it came to pass, when Jacob saw Rachel**
> **the daughter of Laban his mother's brother,**
> **and the sheep of Laban his mother's brother,**
> **that Jacob went near and**
> **rolled the stone from the well's mouth,**
> **and watered the flock of Laban his mother's brother.**
> **Then Jacob kissed Rachel, and**
> **lifted up his voice and wept.**
> **(Genesis 29:10–11 NKJV)**

Jacob, Isaac's son, follows his father in playing the Abrahamic *Dating Game*—and for the same reason—Dad's demand for religious purity only found in unequivocal devotion to the LORD God. The LORD God's men were not to marry idolatrous Canaanite women.

Unlike Isaac, Jacob is given permission to seek the girl of his dreams (within limits) on his own. He sets off merrily to the land of his mom in search of Miss Right. And by now you might guess it. He finds her by a well. A beautiful shepherdess, a vision of loveliness, heaven sent just for Jacob. He tries to maintain some cool, but as you can see, the boy could have been a bit impetuous. It apparently is love at first sight. No script this time. Just eye-popping passion, complete with chivalry, a feat of strength, a first kiss, and tears—the water of uncapped joy.

Jesus said to her [the Samaritan woman],
"Everyone who drinks of this water will be thirsty again,
but whoever drinks of the water
that I will give him will never be thirsty again.
The water that I will give him will become in him a spring of
water welling up to eternal life." (John 4:13–14 NKJV)

Wells and springs are crucial to existence everywhere but especially in the arid Middle East. Perhaps that is why the Word of God shares significant stories about wells and women—both being givers and sustainers of life. Hagar is saved twice through God's water-borne intervention. A covenant of nationhood teetering on extinction is redeemed through the miraculous well provided for her son, Ishmael. Abraham's son Isaac and grandson Jacob discover their wives at wells.

All of scripture exists for a special purpose: to point toward, at, or back to Jesus Christ, the promised savior and rescuer spoken of in the Garden of Eden. In the accounts of the three women at the well, Hagar, Rebekah, and Rachel, Genesis foreshadows the bottomless source of "living water" found only in Jesus and offered freely and without limit.

There is in scripture another significant woman at the well. She is the Samaritan woman at "Jacob's well." She is lonely, cast off, and rejected by ancestry and by life choices. She is a lowly sinner by every human standard but a water carrier to the thirsty. And at Jacob's well she finds herself face to face with the one who alone is sinless—the carrier of living water to the thirsty. Jesus came to save sinners.[38]

Also Isaac's servants dug in the valley,
and found a well of running water there.
But the herdsmen of Gerar
quarreled with Isaac's herdsmen, saying,
"The water is ours."
So he called the name of the well Esek ["contention"],

---

[38] John 4:1–30 and 1 Timothy 1:15.

because they quarreled with him.
(Genesis 26:19–20 NKJV)

"The water is ours." Here we have the plea of modern domestic and international court briefs and the frequent cause of violent conflict. As a bumper sticker, it would have been apt for the donkey cart of Abraham's son, Isaac. Warned by the LORD during famine not to go to Egypt, he found the wells dug in his father's day stopped up by the Philistines. With a bent for peace similar to his father's with nephew Lot, Isaac pulled up stakes and dug another well, which came to be called *Sitnah* ("strife"). As its sad name indicates, the quarreling continued. Only when Isaac dug a third well called Rehoboth ("wide places") did struggles cease. Isaac proceeded then to Beersheba ("well of the sevenfold oath") where the LORD renewed his covenant promise of land and descendants. Isaac responded in amazed gratitude by building an altar and in steadfast covenant faith by digging another well.

He [Jacob] fled with all that he had
and arose and crossed the Euphrates,
and set his face toward the hill country of Gilead.
(Genesis 31:21 ESV)

When last we saw Jacob, he was instantly and deliriously lovesick for want of Rachel, the beautiful shepherdess at Uncle Laban's well. We meet him again many years later—older and wiser. Laban has conned him, after seven years of servitude, into marrying Rachel's far less marketable sister, Leah. In promise of seven more years of work, Laban unlocks Rachel's virtual handcuffs. The second union goes forward. Wedded bliss, no surprise, does not.

Rachel, like Sarah before her, is not prompt in bearing children, a must for self-respect and for social security in an ancient world dependent on strong young workers and child bearers. After Leah births four sons, Rachel remembers Grandma's antidote for nonfertility—farm out her maid. No sooner said than done. Bilbah bears two more sons for the ever-compliant Jacob. Not to be outdone, Leah makes available her maid, Zilpah, who delivers two more boys into Jacob's burgeoning and increasingly contentious household.

If all this were not sufficient motivation for Jacob to cross the Euphrates for a new start, he and Laban continued to be beset by shady business deals as well as related women and son troubles. Enough being too much, Jacob packs up and pulls out.

> **Again she [Leah] conceived and bore a son … called Levi.**
> **And she conceived again and bore a son,**
> **and said, "This time I will praise the LORD."**
> **Therefore she called his name Judah.**
> **Then she ceased bearing. (Genesis 29:34–35 ESV)**

Actually, Leah ceased bearing only for the time being, adding Issachar and Zebulon later. Final son tally: Leah 6, Bilbao 2, Zillah 2, Rachel 2. Rachel's two boys are the final entries, the last one taking her life in childbirth.

Jacob's twelve sons become fathers to the twelve tribes of Israel. One would expect the most influential and well-known of them to be sons of the lovely Rachel. The LORD seldom, if ever, works in Hollywood predictability. It is second fiddle Leah who provides Israel with Levi and Judah. Centuries later the LORD will designate Levi's entire tribe as priestly representative before him. More centuries later, he will raise up from the tribe of Judah the perfect sinless Lamb of God, who makes obsolete all other sacrifice and all other sacrificing priests.

The LORD in decidedly unforeseeable fashion seems to take special interest in rejected women. When Jesus' genealogies are written, the list will include a Canaanite prostitute, Moabite widow, and Israelite mistress to a king, as well as Judah's daughter-in-law unwittingly recruited by him for an act of prostitution ending in incest.[39]

---

[39] Joshua, chapters 2–6; Book of Ruth; 2 Samuel 11–12:24; Genesis 38:6–10; Matthew 1; and Luke 3.

JOSEPH

Then Judah said to his brothers,
"What profit is it if we kill our brother
and conceal his blood?
Come, let us sell him to the Ishmaelites,
and let not our hand be upon him,
for he is our brother, our own flesh."
And his brothers listened to him.

Then Midianite traders passed by.
And they drew Joseph up and lifted him out of the pit,
and sold him to the Ishmaelites
for twenty shekels of silver.
They took Joseph to Egypt. (Genesis 37:26–28 ESV)

Joseph, first born of Jacob's sweetie, Rachel, became Dad's favorite of the twelve. In a family of a dozen boys, this can't be a good thing. We find the guys in this passage prepared to kill the youngster by letting him rot in a dry water pit. Judah, brimming with brotherly compassion, suggests that they merely sell him into slavery.

Why all this animosity? Jacob, in a brilliant move of fatherly wisdom, had made for Joseph a wonderful and colorful robe. None for Reuben, Simeon, etc, etc. Just for Joseph. There's more. Joseph was known to be a tattletale, sharing with Dad the failings of the older guys. All this proved a wonderful incentive for homicide. After all, the guys were shepherds living and working in vast real estate where a little kid could just somehow disappear.

The LORD had something else in mind for little brother, something that would change the course of Hebrew and world history. Through his divine intervention and the very human conniving of Judah, Joseph is pulled from a slow death in the pit. He is hauled away with the rest of the Midianite cargo to Egypt, to the fabulous Nile River and to slavery.

> Now Joseph had been brought down to Egypt,
> and Potiphar, an officer of Pharaoh,
> the captain of the guard, an Egyptian,
> had bought him from the Ishmaelites
> who had brought him down there.
> The LORD was with Joseph,
> and he became a successful man,
> and he was in the house of his Egyptian master.
> (Genesis 39:1–2 ESV)

For a lad, one second thought short of shriveling to death in a dry pit, Joseph fared well in the human trade sweepstakes. He settled in a very soft landing into the household of a very high Egyptian official. In these two short verses, we are informed that as Dorothy in *The Wizard of Oz* would put it, "This isn't Kansas." It is Egypt. Like Oz, Egypt dazzled and glitzed with all the splendors and beauty the ancient world could offer. Like Oz, it lurked of hidden snares and dangers.

And amid the dazzles and the lurks, Joseph was to prosper, fall, and prosper again. And all the while, "the LORD was with Joseph".

> His master saw that the LORD was with him
> and that the LORD caused all that he did
> to succeed in his hands.
> So Joseph found favor in his
> [Potiphar] sight and attended him,
> and he made him overseer of his house
> and put him in charge of all that he had.
> From the time that he made him overseer in his house
> and over all that he had,
> the LORD blessed the Egyptian's house for Joseph's sake;
> the blessing of the LORD was on all that he had,
> in house and field. (Genesis 39:3–5 ESV)

Joseph thrived in Potiphar's house. All that he did was successful. Potiphar noticed. He noticed more than Joseph's faithfulness and industry. He noticed that "the LORD" was with Joseph and that "the LORD" caused all that he did to succeed in his hands. Great Grandpa Abraham had been gifted with a covenant promising land and progeny. Also, through him, all the families of the earth were to be blessed. Until now Abraham's family was hardly a blessing even to itself. Joseph, however, clearly became a blessing to the family, household, and even the fields of Potiphar. The multiblessed Potiphar rewarded Joseph with authority over his entire house. If Joseph remained faithful, what could go wrong?

> **Now Joseph was handsome in form and appearance.**
> **And after a time his master's wife**
> **Cast her eyes on Joseph and said, "Lie with me."**
> **But he refused and said to his master's wife,**
> **"Behold, because of me my master**
> **has no concern about anything in the house,**
> **and he has put everything that he has in my charge.**
> **He is not greater in this house than I am,**
> **nor has he kept back anything from me except**
> **you, because you are his wife.**
> **How then can I do this great wickedness**
> **and sin against God?" (Genesis 39:6–9 ESV)**

More woman problems in Abraham's covenant family.[40] This time it is the woman who is on the prowl, and not with ladylike intent. Joseph, a Biblically proclaimed "looker," catches the lustful eyes of Potiphar's wife. A glance becomes a proposition, and in no uncertain terms. Joseph, in utter loyalty to Potiphar, rebuffs the offer in equal and unequivocal language. He states the immediate reason: How could I be so ungrateful to your husband to whom I owe so much? He adds the underlying fundamental reason: this is wickedness, this is sin. How could I be so ungrateful to God?

Back in the Garden of Eden, God set the terms of marriage: "Therefore a man shall leave his father and his mother and hold fast to his wife, and they

---

[40] See Genesis 38 for brother Judah, back home, falling in attempted prostitution and fulfilled incest.

shall become one flesh" (Genesis 2:24 ESV). Since Eve's fruit in the garden, temptation had not come any juicier. Joseph chose God's way.

> **And Joseph's master took him**
> **and put him into the prison,**
> **the place where the king's prisoners were confined,**
> **and he was there in prison. (Genesis 39:20 ESV)**

By the time God's book, the Bible, is finished, we find a whole lot of his people thrown into one slammer or another for the "crime" of faithfulness to him. Joseph is the first.

Potiphar's wife does not give up easily. Nor does Joseph. She pleads day after day, and he refuses day after day, making every effort not to even be in her presence. Stealthy to the core, she entraps him alone. Joseph makes a run for it and escapes but absent his coat, which she pulls from him. Evidence in hand, scorn matched by fury in her heart, she awaits her husband's return home.

Poor Joseph. So much trouble with robes and coats. And this one not his fault. The testimony of Potiphar's wife, unsurprisingly does not line up with Joseph's. Last time, from the pit, it was rags to riches; now it is riches to rags. No slave wagon this time. An Egyptian prison awaits Jacob's favorite boy.

> **But the LORD was with Joseph**
> **and showed him steadfast love**
> **and gave him favor in the sight of the keeper of the prison.**
> **And the keeper of the prison put Joseph in charge**
> **of all the prisoners who were in the prison.**
> **Whatever was done there, he was the one who did it.**
> **The keeper of the prison paid no attention**
> **to anything that was in Joseph's charge,**
> **because the LORD was with him.**
> **And whatever he did, the LORD made it succeed.**
> **(Genesis 39:21–23 ESV)**

Same song, second verse. "But The LORD was with Joseph and showed him steadfast love and gave him favor in the sight of the keeper of the prison." The LORD and he alone, remained steadfast in Joseph's topsy-turvy life. Joseph finds himself again in the position of trust and privilege. Scripture, as usual, would leave us with no illusion that the ultimate source of good fortune is man, even extraordinary men like Joseph. Not one, but three times in these verses alone, we are informed that in steadfast love "the LORD made it succeed."

"But the LORD" will become a constant companion to times and people caught up in woe, despair, injustice, and uncertainty.

> **And Pharaoh was angry with his two officers,**
> **the chief cupbearer and the chief baker,**
> **and he put them in custody**
> **in the house of the captain of the guard,**
> **in the prison where Joseph was confined.**
> **And one night they both dreamed—**
> **the cupbearer and the baker of the king of Egypt.**
> **(Genesis 40:2–3, 5 ESV)**

Dreams were right up Joseph's alley. They had gotten him in trouble with the older brothers and even his father back in the old country.[41] Jacob's gift of a multicolored robe along with Joseph's tattling tendency were enough to earn him a death sentence. To boot, Joseph had two dreams. In the first, he and his brothers were bundling grain. His bundle stood up, and the brothers' bundles bowed low before it. In another dream, the sun, moon, and eleven stars bowed before him.

Not content to keep his nocturnal entertainment to himself, he reported the first dream to his brothers and the second to Jacob as well as to the brothers. From his father, he received a scolding.

---

[41] Genesis 37:5–11.

Did he actually think that Mom, Dad, and the entire family would bow down on the ground before him? Still, Jacob wondered what this meant. The brothers spent no time wondering and considerable time plotting, hating "all the more" and being "jealous of him."[42]

> **After two whole years,**
> **pharaoh dreamed that he was standing by the Nile,**
> **and behold, there came up out of the Nile**
> **seven cows attractive and plump,**
> **and they fed in the reed grass.**
> **And behold, seven other cows, ugly and thin,**
> **came up out of the Nile after them,**
> **and stood by the other cows on the bank**
> **of the Nile. (Genesis 41:1 ESV)**

Joseph interpreted the dreams to the cupbearer and baker of the king. The cupbearer would be restored to his former position while the baker was to be executed. Both predictions quickly came to pass. Joseph asked the cupbearer to remember him to the king when he assumed again his station in life. The cupbearer forgot, and Joseph remained in prison for another two years.

When the cupbearer heard of the king's dream, he remembered Joseph and commended him as an interpreter of dreams. "Then Pharaoh sent and called Joseph, and they quickly brought him out of the pit. And when he had shaved himself and changed his clothes, he came in before Pharaoh"[43]

> **"It is beyond my power to do this," Joseph replied.**
> **"But God can tell you what it means and set you at ease."**
> **"This will happen just as I have described it,**
> **for God has revealed to Pharaoh**
> **in advance what he is about to do.**

---

[42] Genesis 37:8, 11.

[43] "King" is interchangeable with "pharaoh" in identifying Egypt's monarch.

> The next seven years will be a period of great
> prosperity throughout the land of Egypt.
> But afterward there will be seven years of famine
> so great that all the prosperity will be forgotten in Egypt.
> Famine will destroy the land." (Genesis 41:16, 28–30 NLT)

Joseph ascribes all wisdom and glory to God while assuring pharaoh that God will show pharaoh what he is "about to do."

Pharaoh then discloses to Joseph not one dream but a second one. In the first, seven robust cows emerge from the Nile River and are displaced by seven emaciated ones. The starving ones eat the fatted ones but remain as scrawny as before. In the second dream, seven ears of grain grow in fullness on one stock only to be swallowed up by seven thin ears withered by east winds.

The pharaoh has already called on his magicians to interpret the dreams, and they have failed. Joseph will not and cannot fail. He informs the king why that is so. Interpretation is not of him but of his God. Further encounters featuring agents of idolatry versus God's prophets will produce the same results.

> And Pharaoh said to his servants,
> "Can we find a man like this,
> in whom is the Spirit of God?"
> Then Pharaoh said to Joseph,
> "Since God has shown you all this,
> there is none so discerning and wise as you are.
> You shall be over my house, and all my people
> shall order themselves as you command.
> Only as regards the throne will I be greater than you."
> And Pharaoh said to Joseph, "See, I have set you
> over all the land of Egypt." (Genesis 41:38–41 ESV)

Pharaoh notes that his interpreter is inhabited by something very special, "the Spirit of God." He has not only logically interpreted the dreams but has gone on to prescribe a course of wise action. Pharaoh's administration should be organized in such a way as to gather and store bounty for seven years in order to be prepared for seven years of orderly distribution when the worst arrives.

Pharaoh begins, as God continually honors and rewards, by recognizing him as the source of Joseph's discerning counsel. He follows by appointing Joseph as head of his house, czar of feast and famine, and second only to him in "all the land of Egypt."

Rags back to riches! This time Joseph's robe of supremacy will not be stripped from him.

> **When Jacob learned that there
> was grain for sale in Egypt,
> he said to his sons, "Why do you look at one another?"
> And he said,
> "Behold, I have heard that there is grain for sale in Egypt.
> Go down and buy grain for us there,
> that we may live and not die."
> So ten of Joseph's brothers went down
> to buy grain in Egypt. (Genesis 42:1 ESV)**

A family reunion unique in all human history is about to take place. After many years separate from the brother they sentenced to slavery, ten of the boys are dispatched to Egypt to secure food for Jacob's hungry family. Baby brother Benjamin, the last boy of the flock and son of the favored but late Rachel, stays behind for safekeeping.

Joseph recognizes them though they do not recognize him. Amid tears of joy they never see, he accuses them of being spies but arranges their return home with provisions of food. Brother Simeon is held behind as guarantee that Benjamin will subsequently be sent to Egypt to verify their pleas of innocence. They were not spies but brothers sent on a mission of life or death mercy for an aging father, brother, and sisters.

The story is far more convoluted and brilliantly orchestrated by Joseph than can be accounted here.[44] Its climax is this: the brothers twelve, during repeated bouts of weeping, are reunited with Joseph and sent back with wagons to retrieve dad. Jacob, overcome with initial disbelief, is won over by the moving vans and storage before him and announces, "It must be true! My son Joseph is alive! I must go and see him before I die" (Genesis 45:28 NLT).

> **So Israel [Jacob] took his journey with all that he had**
> **and came to Beersheba,**
> **and offered sacrifices to the God of his father Isaac.**
> **And God spoke to Israel in visions of the night and said,**
> **"Jacob, Jacob."**
> **And he said, "Here I am."**
> **Then he said, "I am God, the God of your father.**
> **Do not be**
> **afraid to go down to Egypt,**
> **for there I will make you into a great nation."**
> **(Genesis 46:1–3 ESV)**

Jacob journeys toward Egypt with all his people and possessions. At Beersheba he stops and sacrifices to the "God of his father Isaac." During the night, God personally assures him that he will find safety in Egypt and that, as guaranteed to his dad and granddad, God will make of him a great nation.

Earlier Isaac, also caught in famine, was told *not* to flee to Egypt. At Beersheba, seeking famine and drought relief, both men sacrificed to God, and both were promised by the unswerving LORD God of Abraham that he will be faithful to his people and his covenant. Beersheba is delightfully named. As the God of creation rested from his labors on the seventh day, so Abraham's son and grandson find rest, as well as assurance, at the "well of the sevenfold oath."

> **Then Pharaoh said to Joseph,**
> **"Your father and your brothers have come to you.**
> **The land of Egypt is before you.**

---

[44] Genesis 42–47.

> Settle your father and your brothers
> in the best of the land.
> Let them settle in the land of Goshen,
> and if you know any able men among them,
> put them in charge of my livestock." (Genesis 47:5–6 ESV)

Jacob arrives safely in Egypt with his large family and corporate enterprise of people and animals. The family is happily reunited, and forgiveness owns the day. Now it is time to get practical. How will they all live and prosper? Time for a good old family "sting operation."

Joseph parlays with the brothers and household, counseling them to inform Pharaoh that they have been "keepers of livestock from our youth even until now, both we and our fathers." Though this be "cross their hearts" true, the statement is designed to lure Pharaoh into a trap that would set up the Hebrews in some mighty fine nomadic real estate. The Egyptians looked upon shepherding as low life. Perhaps Pharaoh would offer the choice piece of land at Goshen and also franchise his own livestock to the oversight of Jacob and sons. Done!

SAVIORS FORESHADOWED

> Now there arose a new king over Egypt,
> who did not know Joseph.
> And he said to his people,
> "Behold, the people of Israel are too many
> and too mighty for us.
> Come, let us deal shrewdly with them, lest they multiply,
> and, if war breaks out, they join our enemies
> and fight against us and escape from the land."
> (Exodus 1:8–10 ESV)

Four hundred and thirty years had passed since Jacob's family had settled in Goshen as sheepherders.[45] The generous landlord-tenant agreement

---

[45] Exodus 12:40.

arranged between Joseph and his pharaoh had lapsed. Lapsed, as well, was Hebrew loyalty to the covenant of the LORD God of Abraham, Isaac, Jacob, and Joseph.

The prophet Ezekiel relates the LORD God's opinion on the matter as follows: "When I chose Israel—when I revealed myself to the descendants of Jacob in Egypt—I took a solemn oath that I, the LORD, would be their God. I took a solemn oath that day that I would bring them out of Egypt to a land I had discovered and explored for them—a good land, a land flowing with milk and honey, the best of all lands anywhere."

"Then I said to them, 'Each of you, get rid of the vile images you are so obsessed with. Do not defile yourselves with the idols of Egypt, for I am the LORD your God.' But they rebelled against me and would not listen. They did not get rid of the vile images they were obsessed with, or forsake the idols of Egypt. Then I threatened to pour out my fury on them to satisfy my anger while they were still in Egypt."[46]

> **Then the king of Egypt said to the Hebrew midwives,**
> **one of whom was named Shiphrah and the other Puah,**
> **"When you serve as midwife to the Hebrew women**
> **and see them on the birthstool,**
> **if it is a son, you shall kill him,**
> **but if it is a daughter, she shall live."**
> **But the midwives feared God**
> **and did not do as the king of Egypt commanded them,**
> **but let the male children live.**
> **(Exodus 1:15–17 ESV)**

Whether to obey "God or Caesar"[47] will turn out to be a long-standing issue for God's people. The "God" side of the equation never changes. He remains, beginning to end, the Singular, Eternal, Preexisting, and Uncreated Being. However— "Caesars"—those who would replace God

---

[46] Ezekiel 20:6–8 (NLT).
[47] Luke 20:19–26.

as the Supreme Being and authority, ably wield some rather fearful and challenging "big sticks."

Immersed in idolatry and hardly up to knuckle sandwiches, the enslaved Hebrews, save two, did as they were told. Shiphrah and Puah become the first unblemished God champions of the Bible. We don't know much about them, but what we do know is all good. The king, facing a possibility of future violent unrest among the Hebrews, personally charges the women with perpetrating the death of all the male newborns. They respond with courage and moral purity. More significant to the biblical narrative is that they "feared God."

Shiphrah and Puah stand out as virtuous, heroic, and unswervingly faithful women amid their less than admirable male counterparts. They will not be the last.

> Now a man from the house of Levi went and
> took as his wife a Levite woman.
> The woman conceived and bore a son,
> and when she saw that he was a fine child,
> she hid him three months.
> When she could hide him no longer,
> She took for him a basket made of bulrushes
> and daubed it with bitumen and pitch.
> She put the child in it and placed it among the reeds
> by the river bank. (Exodus 2:1–3 ESV)

The king of Egypt takes matters out of the merciful hands of Shiphrah and Puah, ordering his people to drown all Hebrew baby boys in the Nile. One infant, from the future priestly tribe of Levi, is first hidden and later floated in the Nile, among the reeds, out of view of the murderers. Only a miracle could save him. It happened. Pharaoh's daughter saw him in the water, took a major fancy to him, and arranged to have him raised in the very home of her dad.

That baby, Moses, would one day introduce God's people to his perfect law and deliver them out of slavery and to the edge of Father Abraham's Promised Land. It remained for yet another full-grown miracle baby, this time God in the flesh, Jesus Christ, to rescue all believers from the bondage of sin and death and to deliver them safely to and through the gates of heaven.[48]

---

[48] John 1:17 ᴱˢⱽ "The law was given through Moses; grace and truth came through Jesus Christ."

PART III

Serenity to Tempest

Still Waters

**The LORD is my shepherd;
I shall not want.
He maketh me to lie down in green pastures
He leadeth me beside the still waters.
(Psalm 23:1–2 KJV)**

Psalm 23 is the "It doesn't get any better than this" psalm. King David of ancient Israel has had his ups and downs with the LORD. It all began with a divinely driven meteoric rise from shepherd to soldier to monarch. His very name is forever linked to the image of the little guy surmounting the insurmountable as he drops the dreaded giant Goliath with just one missile guided from his trusty sling. Along his jarring path of exhilarating victory and deflating defeat he experiences heights and depths of friendship and enmity with the power brokers of his time.

There is more to his biography, much more. David weaves amid his normally impeccable virtue and morality a depth of depravity seldom matched among Bible villains and never equaled in the lives of biblical heroes. And he has the poetic and musical gifts, as well as a heart for the LORD, to reflect brilliantly on both his Doctor Jekyll and his Mr. Hyde.

Here in Psalm 23, David is oblivious to personal power, tragedy, guilt, failure, or even distraction. It's David and his LORD. That's it. The shepherd is content with the Shepherd of Shepherds. The king is safe with the King of Kings.

The LORD's pastures are verdant with all the "daily bread" David could ever need. David, the leader and great hope of a nation reclines, himself merely a sheep in need of a shepherd, under the watchful eye of the LORD beside "still waters."

WASH ME THOROUGHLY

[To the chief musician, a psalm of David]
When Nathan the prophet came unto him,
after he had gone in to Bathsheba.
Have mercy upon me, O God,
according to thy lovingkindness:
according unto the multitude of thy tender
mercies blot out my transgressions.
Wash me thoroughly from mine iniquity,
and cleanse me from my sin.
For I acknowledge my transgressions:
and my sin is ever before me. (Psalm 51:1 KJV)

David, in Psalm 51, stands before the ultimate court of appeals, the heavenly supreme court, God himself. No shepherd this time, but a judge. The serenity of still waters is displaced by the turbulence of guilt and despair. David is up for divine conviction on a number of counts—adultery, murder, and false witness topping the list.[49] How do even kings get mercy for those? Who could possibly be so lovingly kind? It would take a multitude of tender mercies to blot out that kind of transgression. What quantity and quality of water washes away that quality and quantity of transgression? Still waters have been replaced with floods of guilt. The time for sandbags has passed. Can the deluge-battered soul of the king be restored to grace?

---

[49] 2 Samuel 11.

> Wash me thoroughly from my iniquity,
> And cleanse me from my sin.
> For I acknowledge my transgressions,
> And my sin is always before me.
> Against You, You only, have I sinned,
> And done this evil in Your sight—
> That You may be found just when You speak,
> And blameless when You judge.
> Behold, I was brought forth in iniquity,
> And in sin my mother conceived me.
> (Psalm 51:2–5 NKJV)

King David is an early advocate of "confession is good for the soul." He not only acknowledges personal sin in need of "thorough" cleansing but cries out in emotional pain before the guilt that constantly wags its accusatory finger in his face. Then he places iniquity in heavenly, rather than earthly, perspective. If the Singular, Eternal, Preexisting, and Uncreated Being is the standard for absolute goodness and truth, then any human transgression short of that measure must be first and foremost an affront against him. The very commission and recognition of such an offense, David confesses, is by definition an affirmation of God's sole sovereignty in the assignment of guilt and the demand for justice. "Against you and you only have I sinned."

The king adds that his problems with rebellion against God didn't start with an errant glance at a comely woman but with a condition of his very humanity. Sin, since the fall of Adam and Eve, had been transmitted without exception to every baby ever conceived. "Therefore, just as sin came into the world through one man, and death through sin, so death spread to all men because all sinned" (Romans 5:12 ESV).

> Hide your face from my sins, and
> Blot out all my iniquities.
> Create in me a clean heart,
> O God, and renew a right spirit within me.
> Cast me not away from your presence,

> **and take not your Holy Spirit from me.**
> **(Psalm 51:9–11 ESV)**

The center of David's petition for forgiveness lies in the word *create*. It has not been seen in this form since "In the beginning God created the heavens and the earth" back in the first verse of the Bible. Here in Psalms, as in Genesis, it connotes creation of a kind that produces something out of what was formerly nothing. David's heart, mind, and being need not a "do over" but a fresh beginning. There are no spare parts or remnants within his nature worthy of a remodel. A brand new David, not a used and refurbished David, is in order if there is to be harmony with the Singular, Eternal, Preexisting, and Uncreated Being.

Out of the line of King David will come yet another King of the Jews, Jesus Christ. He too will speak of true repentance and reconciliation with God as coming through *barah*—fresh creation of a new thing from that which previously did not exist. He will call it rebirth. Unlike David, this king will not be in the business of pleading for *barah*. He will be the agent by which *barah*—rebirth, reconciliation of sinners with sinless God, is offered "Most assuredly, I say to you, unless one is born again, he cannot see the kingdom of God." (John 3:3 NKJV "I am the way, the truth, and the life. No one comes to the Father except through me." (John 14:6 NKJV)

> **Purge me with hyssop, and I shall be clean;**
> **Wash me, and I shall be whiter than snow.**
> **Make me hear joy and gladness,**
> **That the bones You have broken may rejoice.**
> **Hide Your face from my sins,**
> **And blot out all my iniquities.**
> **Create in me a clean heart, O God,**
> **And renew a steadfast spirit within me.**
> **(Psalm 51:7–10 NKJV)**

King David, flattened in grief and remorse, recognizes that nothing short of a thorough purging of his very being will return him to "joy and gladness". This is no "wash your hands and face" or "get in the shower." His filth is from within, and nothing short of a 100 percent soapy *barah* wash and rinse will purge him and leave him standing guiltless "whiter than snow" before his God.

The third book of the Bible, Leviticus, prescribes to the priestly class the criteria for appealing for remission of sins. Consistent with ancient concepts of justice, sacrificial blood must be spilled, and ceremonial waters of cleansing must be administered. God's standards for considering forgiveness are high. Leviticus permeates and drips with the words "sacrifice," "wash," and "clean" The first occupies 4.3 percent of its entire contents, the second, 3.5 percent, and the third 4.7 percent. David, recognizing the gravity of his transgressions, bypasses the clergy and goes straight to the LORD God directly, appealing to a mercy not known among mortals.

Snow is a word, understandably, used seldom in the Bible. Only on rare occasions does the white stuff fall even in the elevated city of Jerusalem. However, its pristine beauty has made an impression on the poet, David. Its whiteness connotes to him a spiritual purity representative of a clean heart and a clean start before the Singular, Eternal, Preexisting, and Uncreated Being—a spiritual purity he can yet possess.

> O LORD, open my lips,
> And my mouth shall show forth Your praise.
> For You do not desire sacrifice,
> or else I would give *it*;
> You do not delight in burnt offering.
> The sacrifices of God are a broken spirit,
> A broken and a contrite heart—
> These, O God, You will not despise.
> (Psalm 51:15–17 NKJV)

As King David nears the end of his poem and song, he spills out some rather astonishing words: "You do not desire sacrifice" or "delight in burnt offering." So what about the exhaustive instruction to the priests about the blood of unblemished animals and the proper preparation and burning of their bodies? What about all the washing and cleansing to make the priests and the tools of sacrifice presentable? It turns out something is far more important to God—the broken and contrite heart that longs for forgiveness and restoration.

> **[A psalm of David, a contemplation]**
> **Blessed is he whose transgression is forgiven,**
> **whose sin is covered.**
> **Blessed is the man to whom**
> **the LORD does not impute iniquity,**
> **And in whose spirit there is no deceit.**
> **When I kept silent, my bones grew old through my**
> **groaning all the day long. (Psalm 32:1–3 NKJV)**

King David, the flawed forerunner of the faultless Savior, Jesus Christ, here demonstrates, in yet another poetic song, that he is centuries ahead of his time. Through the priestly mediation of personal and national transgression, it was *un*intentional sin that stood a chance of divine remission.[50]

The king had acted on his lustful, voluntary, premeditated impulses in committing adultery with the attractive married neighbor girl, Bathsheba. To make matters worse, Bathsheba was the wife of one of his most trusted warriors, Uriah, whom he was to order be clandestinely murdered.[51]

David does not escape the divine consequences of his depravity. He loses the child born of the liaison as well as the opportunity to build a temple to his beloved LORD. Still he possesses the supreme audacity to plead forgiveness, and the paramount God-inspired confidence to proclaim it a done deal. If there was any doubt in Psalm 51 that even the most abhorrent of sin can be forgiven the intentional and supreme royal debaucher and cad erases that doubt in Psalm 32. "Blessed is the man to whom the LORD does not impute inquity."

> **When I kept silent, my bones grew old**
> **through my groaning all the day long.**

---

[50] Numbers 15:25–31.
[51] 2 Samuel 11.

> For day and night Your hand was heavy upon me;
> My vitality was turned into the drought of summer. Selah
> I acknowledged my sin to You,
> And my iniquity I have not hidden.
> I said, "I will confess my transgressions to the LORD,"
> And You forgave the iniquity of my sin. Selah.
> For this cause everyone who is godly shall pray to You
> In a time when You may be found; Surely in a flood
> of great waters They shall not come near him.
> (Psalm 32:3–6 NKJV)

The king transmits to the singers of Psalm 32 the agony of unconfessed and unforgiven sin. He has groaned all day before his guilt, shame, and imminent judgment. His life vitality is sapped. Rainless spiritual drought has drained him of life. No more! He has turned to the one who alone can and will forgive and revive. He announces his absolute jaw-dropping assurance of pardon and then reminds his singers to themselves stop and reflect ["Selah"]. Have you really absorbed the profound call to response of what you have just sung? Sin, even of the unspeakable brand, can be and will be forgiven when offered before the throne of the LORD with a broken, contrite, repentant heart. Contemplate deeply, implores the royal song master, before singing on.

> I acknowledged my sin to You,
> And my iniquity I have not hidden.
> I said, "I will confess my transgressions to the LORD,"
> And You forgave the iniquity of my sin. Selah.
> For this cause everyone who is godly shall pray to You
> In a time when You may be found;
> Surely in a flood of great waters
> They shall not come near him. (Psalm 32:5–6 NKJV)

King David doesn't pull punches in his confession of sin to the LORD. He describes it as "iniquity," in Hebrew a word for "depravity" and "perversity." He places both his confession and the LORD's forgiveness in the past tense—darkest sin and dazzling amazing grace—both a done deal.

And now the poet king takes up a cause. He calls all who would be godly to lay their own astonishing sin before an infinitely more astonishing forgiver who seeks that he may be found—not tomorrow but today, the acceptable time.[52]

David, the sinner supreme, has somehow foreseen his descendant, Jesus Christ, the Son of God, "the Lamb of God who takes away the sin of the world." [53] He invites anyone willing to sing his song to its finish to a front row view of the Savior. Selah.

HE WILL COME TO US LIKE THE RAIN

Come, and let us return to the LORD;
For He has torn, but He will heal us;
He has stricken, but He will bind us up.
After two days He will revive us;
On the third day He will raise us up,
That we may live in His sight.
Let us know, Let us pursue the knowledge of the LORD.
His going forth is established as the morning;
He will come to us like the rain,
Like the latter and former rain to the earth.
(Hosea 6:1–3 NKJV)

God raised up many a prophet to call his people back to the love affair with him that he so deeply desired and that David so emotionally extolled. It was a prophet, Nathan, who called David, the king, back to "a right relationship" with his maker and redeemer. Prophets from Hosea to Malachi would leave their own Old Testament books for all to read. It would be they and unpublished but Biblically recorded prophets Elisha, Elijah, and others who plead with bullheaded and idolatrous future kings and subjects to turn from their wicked ways.

---

[52] Jeremiah 29:14, Psalm 69:13, Isaiah 49:8, 2 Corinthians 6:2.
[53] John 1:36.

And few could refrain from calling up the powerful image of H_2O—God's never failing King of Chemistry and reigning biblical monarch of metaphors. As the superlative imagery of divine mercy and peace as well as judgment and course correction, it knows no peers.

The LORD says Hosea, will "come to us like the rain."

> **I am the LORD your God ever since the land of Egypt,**
> **And you shall know no God but Me;**
> **For there is no Savior besides Me.**
> **I knew you in the wilderness, In the land of great drought.**
> **When they had pasture, they were filled;**
> **They were filled and their heart was exalted;**
> **Therefore they forgot Me. (Hosea 13:4–6 NKJV)**

The prophet Hosea is speaking to the ten northern tribes of Hebrews who have pivoted 180 degrees from love and worship of him and from active compassion for others. They, along with the remaining two tribes, had been rescued from the pharaoh and enslavement. The LORD, their God, had sustained them and their flocks and herds during forty nomadic years in the drought-ridden desert prior to their reaching the land promised to Abraham. In return for filled bellies and watered throats, he receives the bended knee of idolatry that always flows from self-satisfied bodies, hearts, and minds oblivious to their sole source of provision.

The LORD, though "merciful and gracious and abounding in steadfast love,"[54] has finally had enough. Hosea likens him to a lion or to a leopard lurking by the road. To grasp fully the magnitude of God's righteous anger toward rejection in the face of unparalleled love and provision, Hosea compares his wrath to that of a bear deprived of her cubs.

However, as is the LORD's custom in chastising his errant flock, he reminds them that the final victory is his. "You shall know no other God but me." As for any hope, "There is no savior besides me."

---

[54] Psalm 103:8[ESV]

ELIJAH

**Now Elijah said to Ahab,
"As the LORD, the God of Israel, lives,
before whom I stand,
there shall be neither dew nor rain these years,
except by my word." (1 Kings 17:1 NKJV)**

At the LORD God's word, the prophet Elijah adventures through drought in a most interesting manner. He drinks from the brook Cherith for a time and is provided bread and meat morning and evening by ravens. Brooks without rain, however, have a way of drying up. The Cherith was no exception. Elijah proceeds to the town of Zarephath, where he encounters a widow at the city gate. He requests her to give him some water and a piece of bread. She responds that she is gathering sticks for fuel to prepare a last meal for her dying son. Undeterred, he informs her that this is God's errand. She is to give him a cake of bread and then cook for herself and her son from jars of oil and flour that shall never be empty throughout the drought. The miracle accomplished, her gratitude turns to contempt when her son takes ill and dies. Amid his own dismay, he calls upon the LORD three times to "let this child's life return to him." His prayer is answered. The widow's son is restored and returned to her.[55] The LORD has used Elijah to miraculously demonstrate his power over nature and death.

Another challenge, this one from the idolatrous powers of spiritual darkness, waits in the wings.

**When Ahab saw Elijah, Ahab said to him,
"Is it you, you troubler of Israel?"
And he answered, "I have not troubled Israel,
but you have, and your father's house, because you have
abandoned the commandments of the LORD
and followed the Baals." (1 Kings 18:17–18 ESV)**

---

[55] 1 Kings 17.

The Northern Kingdom of Hebrews may have lacked for water, but never was it short of unfaithful kings. Ahab and his wife, Jezebel, topped the list. "Surely there was no one like Ahab who sold himself to do evil in the sight of the LORD, because Jezebel his wife incited him."[56]

The king and queen have aligned themselves with the notorious god Baal, often depicted as a powerful bull, and his wife, Asherah. In prelude to a battle for the ages, Elijah plucks the chip off the king's rebellious shoulder and commands to Mount Carmel "the 450 prophets of Baal and 400 prophets of the Asherah, who eat at Jezebel's table." Ahab not only picks up the gauntlet but notifies his people to show up for a skirmish to the finish.

At Mount Carmel, Elijah calls for two bulls to be picked out by the prophets of Baal. They may choose one for themselves, cut it up, and lay it on the wood of the altar unlighted. Elijah will do the same with the other animal. Elijah may have been Ahab's "troubler of Israel," but the king is about to find out what "trouble" really is.

> **And you call upon the name of your god,**
> **and I will call upon the name of the LORD,**
> **and the God who answers by fire, he is God."**
> **And all the people answered,**
> **"It is well spoken." (1 Kings 18:25 ESV)**

What an ingenious challenge. Only a real God could pull this one off. The crowd, taking on the role of cheerleader, anticipates that the good times are about to roll. What splendid entertainment this will be.

"O Baal, answer us!" But there was no voice, and no one answered. And they limped around the altar that they had made. At noon Elijah mocked them, saying, "Cry aloud, for he is a god. Either he is musing, or he is relieving himself, or he is on a journey, or perhaps he is asleep and must be awakened." "Relieving himself?" Elijah is near giddy with ridicule. The prophets of Baal

---

[56] 1 Kings 21:25.

are not done, though. "And they cried aloud and cut themselves after their custom with swords and lances, until the blood gushed out upon them."

Noonday passes, and they "rave on." No one answered; no one paid attention. Ahab's best scrappers have thrown their wildest jabs, uppercuts, and haymakers into the wind.[57] What does the LORD have in Elijah's bare fist for the final round? The challengers slouch exhausted in their corner as the bell is about to ring.

> **And Elijah came near to all the people and said,**
> **"How long will you go limping**
> **between two different opinions?**
> **If the LORD is God, follow him;**
> **but if Baal, then follow him."**
> **And the people did not answer him a word.**
> **(1 Kings 18:21 ESV)**

The entire event had been preceded by the above challenge from Elijah. The primary problem God's people had and continued to have is not so much denying the LORD but gradually diluting him. There was and is a recurrent tendency to hedge the bets. Maybe a merger is in order, they conjecture. It couldn't hurt to stir in a bit of a Baal or Asheroth or Molek or Dagan to the worship stew. Very few modern believers get up early for Baal's sunrise service. However, money, youth, sex, ambition, work, health, friends, entertainment … they constitute a more complicated challenge in terms of casting a vote for the Singular, Eternal, Preexisting, and Uncreated Being who is also the one and only LORD God.

The LORD lays down rather succinctly his viewpoint on divided loyalty in the last book of the Bible. The crucified, resurrected, and ascended to heaven Jesus Christ, the Son of God, asserts, "I know your works: you are neither cold nor hot. Would that you were either cold or hot. So, because you are lukewarm, and neither hot nor cold, I will spit you out of my mouth." Revelation 3:16 (ESV).

---

[57] 1 Kings 18:20–29.

> Then Elijah said to all the people,
> "Come near to me." And all the people came near to him.
> And he repaired the altar of the LORD
> that had been thrown down.
> Elijah took twelve stones, according
> to the number of the tribes of the sons of Jacob,
> to whom the word of the LORD came,
> saying, "Israel shall be your name,"
> and with the stones he built an altar
> in the name of the LORD.
> And he made a trench about the altar.
> (1 Kings 18:30–32 ESV)

Most of the day has passed. Ahab's cheerleaders, the people of his kingdom, are likely asleep or quite distracted from the waning groans of the wounded and dispirited prophets. Elijah pulls them aside. "Come near to me." What he didn't say, but what any lesser, non-gloating mortal probably would have, is, "Watch this."

Elijah starts over, building an altar untarnished by false worship and prayer. Reminding the people that they and the LORD had a solemn, unconditional deal, he constructs his altar from twelve stones representing the covenant tribes of Jacob. Quite dramatic in impact, one can be sure. But what about the trench? Wouldn't that imply lots of water? And aren't we in a drought?

Is this one of those old-time movie serials? The endangered hero needs some heroics. Come back next week to see the exciting conclusion.

> And he put the wood in order
> and cut the bull in pieces and laid it on the wood.
> And he said, "Fill four jars with water and
> pour it on the burnt offering and on the wood."
> And he said, "Do it a second time."
> And they did it a second time. And he said,
> "Do it a third time." And they did it a third time.

> **And the water ran around the altar and filled the**
> **trench also with water. (1 Kings 18:33–35 ESV)**

Watch this! Your prophets bit the drought-provided dust. And you have chosen to waver. Watch this! Fill four jars of water and pour it over the wood and partitioned bull. Do it again. Do it again. Watch this! The water "ran around the altar and filled the trench."

The LORD God has a special thing for the number twelve. He placed the future of his covenant relationship first in the hands of twelve chosen tribes, then in the care of twelve handpicked disciples. Here he teases the rapt attention of all by ordering just four douses of water on the sacrifice. Now go get four more and pour those! Not enough, four more! How clever! Four plus four plus four = twelve. That just happens to equal the number of tribes with which I, your I Am, was supposed to have an unconditional deal.

What on earth could make the point better than that? Or what … from heaven?

> **At the usual time for offering the evening sacrifice,**
> **Elijah the prophet walked up to the altar and prayed,**
> **"O LORD, God of Abraham, Isaac, and Jacob,**
> **prove today that you are God in Israel**
> **and that I am your servant.**
> **Prove that I have done all this at your command.**
> **O LORD, answer me! Answer me so these people**
> **will know that you, O LORD, are God**
> **and that you have brought them back to yourself."**
> **(1 Kings 18:36–37 NLT)**

Just in case the people of Israel had missed the object lesson, Elijah reminds them just who this LORD is. He is the God of Israel, the twelve tribes, including these ten, the chosen people of covenant.

And just in case they had forgotten those details in their rush to "unchoose" *him*, Elijah requests a demonstration, a proof that he is the prophet. He is not just one more fly-by-night hustler but the servant of the holy one of Israel.

Elijah calls out twice for proof and twice for an answer to the Mount Carmel challenge. Why? So none will miss the point of the demonstration to come. That the LORD is the God of Israel, that Elijah is his true prophet and that he is about to, beyond all standards of known justice, restore his people to himself.

> **Then the fire of the LORD fell**
> **and consumed the burnt offering**
> **and the wood and the stones and the dust,**
> **and licked up the water that was in the trench.**
> **And when all the people saw it,**
> **they fell on their faces and said,**
> **"The LORD, he is God; the LORD, he is God."**
> **(1 Kings 18:38–39 ESV)**

Nothing was or is able to withstand the justice of the I Am. Steer flesh, wood, stone, dust, and water all are eaten by his mighty flames. The insatiable fire consumes all, licking the water to the last drop. Object lessons abound in the ashes. Idols, constructed by hand from wood and stones, born from dust and dead in dust, exist only by the permission of the I Am. Their demise is but a strike of a match to him.

Who else must be consumed by his righteous anger?

There would be no hope for the deceivers. Their sin had crossed the point of no return. The people of Israel, however, are to be given yet another chance among many. Their road back begins flat on their faces in recognition, at last, of who it is that they have ditched for the company of counterfeits.

> **And Elijah said to them, "Seize the prophets of Baal;**
> **Let not one of them escape."**
> **And they seized them.**
> **And Elijah brought them down**

> to the brook Kishon and slaughtered them there.
> And Elijah said to Ahab, "Go up, eat and drink,
> for there is a sound of the rushing of rain."
> So Ahab went up to eat and to drink.
> And Elijah went up to the top of Mount Carmel.
> And he bowed himself down on the earth and
> put his face between his knees. (1 Kings 18:40–42 ESV)

Those who hold that "the punishment should fit the crime" will be struck by the irony in the deaths of the prophets of Baal. They who could not coax their lifeless gods to bring rain breathed their last in a stream called the Brook Kishon, likely swollen by the downpour on Mount Carmel. It was there, fittingly, in an earlier time of idolatry that an Israelite woman named Deborah rose up to lead the defeat of the idolatrous Canaanite king, Jabin.[58]

As for Ahab, in what seems a mocking, Elijah invites Ahab to ascend the mountain of his defeat and drink up. The trash talk concludes with a reminder of the obvious, "There is the sound of rushing rain." Did Ahab drink first and then bow his humiliated self "down on the earth and put his face between his knees" or were those events in reverse. We are not told. But in any case, like his prophets before him, his final judgment looms.

> Ahab told Jezebel all that Elijah had done,
> and how he had killed all the prophets with the sword.
> Then Jezebel sent a messenger to Elijah, saying,
> "So may the gods do to me and more also,
> if I do not make your life as the life of one of them
> by this time tomorrow." (1 Kings 19:1–2 ESV)

Ahab's wife, Jezebel, a symbol in the book of Revelation for the evil of end-times,[59] is none too pleased with the king's current events report. She vows to do in the prophet Elijah or die at the hands of the defeated gods to whom she yet clings.

---

[58] Judges 4. See also Judges 5 for Deborah's song of victory.
[59] Revelation 20-23

Elijah gets the message and flees in fear and also in concern for the rebellious people of Israel. He arrives at Beersheba, where Abraham had once lived and Isaac had made covenant with the LORD at the "well of the sevenfold oath." More water ... and more to come. In an encounter with an angel, Elijah is given water and hot bread. He attempts sleep but is awakened again to food and drink and sent on his way to a forty-day fast on Mount Horeb, where the LORD God had given another prophet, Moses, the Ten Commandments. There, at the entrance of a cave, he encounters the LORD, who asks what he is doing there.

> He said, "I have been very jealous
> for the LORD, the God of hosts.
> For the people of Israel have forsaken your covenant,
> thrown down your altars,
> and killed your prophets with the sword,
> and I, even I only, am left,
> and they seek my life, to take it away."
> (1 Kings 19:10 ESV)

It is not only the fear of Jezebel and those who kill the prophets that ignites Elijah's answer to the LORD but a sense of despair over his idolatrous people and of downright discouragement in the lonely, dangerous road he walks. He prefers death and conveys that to the LORD, who, as often is the case, has other ideas. He will raise up Ahab's demise in the form of a powerful Syrian army. And the weary Elijah is authorized to anoint his successor, Elisha, to ultimately carry on the labors.

Elijah is not finished yet. And neither is Ahab, who wins some military victories over the next years. His downfall will be over an issue of justice.

> Even though you offer me your
> burnt offerings and grain offerings,
> I will not accept them; and
> the peace offerings of your fattened animals,
> I will not look upon them.
> Take away from me the noise of your songs;

> **to the melody of your harps I will not listen.**
> **But let justice roll down like waters, and righteousness**
> **like an ever-flowing stream. (Amos 5:22–24 ESV)**

Amos, called out of shepherding to be a prophet to the ten tribes of the Northern Kingdom, echoes a theme from another promoted shepherd, King David. The LORD is not interested in even the most meticulously prepared sacrifice if it is not offered with a contrite and broken heart resolved to repentance.

Amos cites, in his book, the oppression of the poor and crushing of the needy. He reminds offenders that the LORD God has ways of dealing with this, including the withholding of the fruit of the skies. "I also withheld rain from you, when there were still three months to the harvest. I made it rain on one city; I withheld rain from another city. One part was rained upon, and where it did not rain the part withered."

The people of Amos's day showed themselves as stiff-necked as those of Elijah's. The LORD continues, "So two or three cities wandered to another city to drink water, but they were not satisfied; yet you have not returned to me." [60]

The LORD is weary of the offerings and even the songs. "Let justice," he declares, "roll down like waters, and righteousness like an ever-flowing stream." It is in humans acting justly toward him and toward their neighbors that the LORD is pleased. In the absence of that justice, his own rivers, as at Mount Carmel, will most assuredly roll.

Case in point: Ahab and the vineyard of Naboth.

> **Now Naboth the Jezreelite had a vineyard in Jezreel,**
> **beside the palace of Ahab king of Samaria.**
> **And after this Ahab said to Naboth,**
> **"Give me your vineyard,**

---

[60] Amos 4:7–8.

> that I may have it for a vegetable garden,
> because it is near my house,
> and I will give you a better vineyard for it;
> or, if it seems good to you,
> I will give you its value in money." (1 Kings 21:1–2 ESV)

King Ahab makes an offer on a vineyard adjacent to his palace owned by a commoner. Rebuffed in his bid, the king returns to the throne to sulk. His bride, Jezebel, is not so easily spurned and arranges Naboth's execution on the pretext of his having cursed God (whoever that may be in her eyes) and the king.

The execution is carried out by stoning, prompting the LORD to have Elijah pay a return visit to the king. He informs Ahab that he will die "because you have sold yourself to do what is evil in the sight of the LORD."[61]

> And you shall say to him, 'Thus says the LORD,
> "Have you killed and also taken possession?"
> And you shall say to him,
> Thus says the LORD:
> "In the place where dogs licked up the blood of Naboth
> shall dogs lick your own blood." (1 Kings 21:19 ESV)

King Ahab has survived three years since the Battle at Mount Carmel. He has won significant battles against the Syrians. But his demise is now assured, and it will come in battle. An errant spear penetrates his armor, and he quits the battle to get about dying. He was in Samaria. "His chariot was washed by the pool of Samaria, and the dogs licked up his blood, and the prostitutes washed themselves in it, according to the word of the LORD that he had spoken."[62]

---

[61] 1 Kings 21:20.
[62] 1 Kings 22:31–38.

And wife Jezebel? "In the territory of Jezreel the dogs shall eat the flesh of Jezebel, and the corpse of Jezebel shall be as dung on the face of the field in the territory of Jezreel, so that no one can say, this is Jezebel."[63]

To cap it all, the LORD empowers King Jehu of the Northern Kingdom to strike "down all who remained of the house of Ahab in Jezreel, all his great men and his close friends and his priest."[64]

JOB

"Why did I not die at birth?
Why did I not perish when I came from the womb?"
(Job 3:11 NKJV)

In the beloved 1946 movie *A Wonderful Life*, family man and reluctant banker George Bailey yearns to never have lived when his hopes and dreams dissipate in a sudden whirlwind of economic disaster. George is ultimately rescued, and his despair is turned to joy by an otherwise inept angel named Clarence.

"Job" names a man as well as the oldest book in the Bible. He too pines for nonexistence. Job is the timeless and universal test case of a good man whom life has taken far beyond the ability of his heart and mind to manage. He has lost much more than his financial security. He has lost his entire wealth, his children, and his health. To boot, his Clarences turn out to be well-meaning but also inept friends who are quite confident and eager to share with Job their misguided and mistaken philosophical viewpoints on the matter.

It turns out, as all symposiums do, that there are no easy answers to why people suffer, especially good people like George and Job. But each discovers his life has meaning and purpose in the eyes of God. In the unfolding of Job's enlightenment, we learn a lot about God's sovereignty—his unmatched

---

[63] 1 Kings 9:36,37
[64] 2 Kings 10:11.

wisdom in running his universe. In the process he will disclose a good deal about his King of Chemistry—water.

> **There was a man in the land of Uz, whose name was Job;**
> **and that man was blameless and upright,**
> **and one who feared God and shunned evil.**
> **And seven sons and three daughters were born to him.**
> **Also, his possessions were**
> **seven thousand sheep, three thousand camels,**
> **five hundred yoke of oxen, five hundred female**
> **donkeys, and a very large household,**
> **so that this man was the**
> **greatest of all the people of the East.**
> **(Job 1:1 NKJV)**

Job: "blameless and upright, and one who feared God, and shunned evil." You can't do much better than that. And God appears to have very adequately rewarded Job. Abundant in sons and daughters, he is well set for his golden years when social security will be paid out in the provision and labors of the younger generation. Thousands of animals and a great many servants round out his business inventory. The future is nothing but bright for the "greatest of all people in the east." The sun shines both bright but blessedly droughtless in the land of Uz.

Unknown to Job, however, a bargain has been struck in the heavenlies. Satan taunts the LORD with an assertion that even Job, the best of the best, will cave and curse God if his divine hedge of protection is removed. Satan is allowed to deprive Job of anything but his very personhood in the form of life or health. The tempter and deceiver heads eagerly to the task. Job's children, for whom he has prayed and sacrificed, are wiped out as well as his corps of servants and herds of animals. Job's home is destroyed, as well, by a "great wind." [65]

---

[65] Job 1:1–19.

> Then Job arose, tore his robe, and shaved his head;
> and he fell to the ground and worshiped.
> And he said:
> "Naked I came from my mother's womb,
> And naked shall I return.
> The LORD gave, and the LORD has taken away;
> Blessed be the name of the LORD."
> In all this Job did not sin nor charge God
> with wrong. (Job 1:20–22 RSV)

Job drops to the ground, not in rage, but in worship, leaving us with perspective for the ages. None of us came into this world with anything and none are going out with anything. As it is said in modern terms, "There is no U-Haul behind the hearse". "The LORD gave and the LORD has taken away." Past tense. It's done. He did it. It's his sovereignty, not mine. "Blessed be the name of the LORD."

"In all this, Job did not sin." However, when it rains, it often pours. It's not over.

> The LORD said to Satan,
> "Have you considered my servant Job, that there is none
> like him on the earth, a blameless and upright man,
> who fears God and turns away from evil?
> He still holds fast his integrity,
> although you moved me against him,
> to destroy him without cause."
> Then Satan answered the LORD, "Skin for skin!
> All that a man has he will give for his life.
> But put forth thy hand now,
> and touch his bone and his flesh,
> and he will curse thee to thy face."
> And the LORD said to Satan,
> "Behold, he is in your power; only spare his life."
> (Job 2:3–6 Revised Standard Version)

The ante is officially upped. Satan is given leave to afflict Job in his very flesh. His only restriction—take not his life, a life which, we already know, the long and patiently suffering Job will soon come to rue.

An old saying is often casually dished out for consumption. "As long as you have your health, you have everything." Invariably that line is blurbed glibly by a man or woman who possesses far more than his or her health. For Job, the proverb is very nearly true. His only remaining solace other than health is his wife. He is about to lose the former and be challenged by the latter.

Satan, the mischief maker supreme, has been granted a very long leash from which to perform. Like a panting, tongue-dripping Labrador, he departs for earth eager to stretch that leash to its limit and retrieve that which he regards as rightfully his.

> **So Satan went out from the presence of the LORD,**
> **and struck Job with painful boils from the sole**
> **of his foot to the crown of his head.**
> **And he took for himself a potsherd**[66]
> **with which to scrape himself**
> **while he sat in the midst of the ashes.**
> **Then his wife said to him,**
> **"Do you still hold fast to your integrity?**
> **Curse God and die!" (Job 2:7–9 NKJV)**

One has only to recall the discomfort of a canker sore or a minor cut to feel Job's agony. A whole body covered with boils! Now he has no wealth, no future and, decidedly, no health. His wife, unwittingly, urges him to do just what Satan wants—curse God.

From human measurement of life worth living Job has failed the standard. Wealth and health gone. Even appearance trashed. The bloom is surely off the rose. One translation of this passage calls the sores "loathsome." What "happily ever after" can be in store for Mr. and Mrs. Job? A normal

---

[66] Piece of broken pottery.

marriage? His pain cannot even allow for a compassionate hug from his life mate.

Whether the little lady's advice has come from sympathy, horror, or self-interest cannot be discerned. What can be known is that she will be flabbergasted at his response.

> **Then his wife said to him,**
> **"Do you still hold fast to your integrity?**
> **Curse God and die!"**
> **But he said to her,**
> **"You speak as one of the foolish women speaks.**
> **Shall we indeed accept good from God,**
> **and shall we not accept adversity?"**
> **In all this Job did not sin with his lips. (Job 2:9–10 NKJV)**

Mrs. Job poses a fascinating question to her beleaguered husband. "Do you still hold fast to your integrity?" *Integrity*, a fraternal twin of *integration*, carries the sense of that which is unified, held together, in oneness. You, Job, are the very image of physical, financial, and familial *dis*integration.

If Job was clinging to his integrity by a thread, his wife may have been able to empathize, maybe even buy in, and perhaps throw out a rope. Poor guy! But it is not a slippery grasp she witnesses. Job's fingers have not been pried loose by adversity. His grip, obeying a heart, soul, mind, and strength for God, only grows stronger.[67]

After categorizing his wife's counsel as "foolish," Job states his position. The Singular, Eternal, Preexisting, and Uncreated Being has the right to do what the Singular, Eternal, Preexisting, and Uncreated Being pleases. You didn't seem to have a problem when he lavished unheard of blessings upon us. Ought we not to accept adversity, as well?

---

[67] Mark 12:30.

That is a question, apparently, profound enough to close the mouth of the Mrs. However, to Job's ultimate dismay, reinforcements are on their way to Uz.

> **Now when Job's three friends**
> **Heard of all this adversity that had come upon him,**
> **each one came from his own place—**
> **Eliphaz the Temanite, Bildad the Shuhite,**
> **and Zophar the Naamathite.**
> **For they had made an appointment together to come**
> **and mourn with him, and to comfort him.**
> **And when they raised their eyes from afar,**
> **and did not recognize him,**
> **they lifted their voices and wept;**
> **and each one tore his robe and**
> **sprinkled dust on his head toward heaven.**
> **So they sat down with him on the ground**
> **seven days and seven nights,**
> **and no one spoke a word to him,**
> **for they saw that his grief was very great.**
> **(Job 2:11–13 NKJV)**

Eliphaz, Bildad, and Shuhite start well. Their style could serve as "look here" in an etiquette manual. They do not barge in upon grief and despair but methodically plan out and agree on a mission of mourning and comfort. On sighting Job, they are surely repulsed and saddened.

Their well-crafted plan caves to raw emotion. They dampen the ground with their anguished tears. Afterward, rather than allow Job to see their horror and dismay, each one, from a distance, "tore his robe and sprinkled dust on his head toward heaven."

Then, and only then, they came to Job in likely the superior of all bedside manners—no words. It doesn't last.

{Eliphaz:} "Yet man is born to trouble, As the sparks fly upward.
But as for me, I would seek God, And to
God I would commit my cause—
Who does great things, and unsearchable,
Marvelous things without number.
He gives rain on the earth,
And sends waters on the fields." (Job 5:7–10 NKJV)

{Bilbad:} "The godless seem like a lush plant growing in the sunshine,
its branches spreading across the garden.
Its roots grow down through a pile of stones;
it takes hold on a bed of rocks.
But when it is uprooted, it's as though it
never existed!" (Job 8:16–19 NLT)

{Zophar:} "Can you solve the mysteries of God?
Can you discover everything about the Almighty?
Such knowledge is higher than the heavens—
and who are you?
It is deeper than the underworld—what do you know?
It is broader than the earth and wider than the sea."

For Job, after seven days, enough has finally become too much. Satan had predicted he would pronounce a curse. He does—not upon God, however, but on the day of his birth. This is the cue for his friends to file commentary on matters of life, death, and suffering.

Their counsel as seen above is loaded with water imagery, all designed to demonstrate Job's ignorance of the ways of God and their certainty of their friend's sinfulness and unconfessed guilt.

He has thrown me into the mud.
I'm nothing more than dust and ashes.
I cry to you, O God, but you don't answer.
I stand before you, but you don't even look.
You have become cruel toward me.

> You use your power to persecute me.
> You throw me into the whirlwind
> and destroy me in the storm.
> (Job 30:19–22 NLT)

Job endures "friendly" indictment of all manner: pride, injustice, godlessness, unconfessed sin, false wisdom. He's got them all. The virtuous, all-knowing trio has none. Bilbad sums up their collective plan of action for him: "If you will seek God and plead with the almighty for mercy, if you are pure and upright, surely then he will rouse himself for you and restore your rightful habitation."[68]

Job is neither ready to confess to a sin or sins he cannot find in himself, pleasing the "friends," nor is he prepared to curse his God, exhilarating Satan. He is content, however, to rail at God, who is apparently away without leave. Job draws from the always bubbling spring of watery vocabulary to paint himself as a composite of mud, dust, and ashes, powerless before the whirlwind of stormy destruction.

> "God alone understands the way to wisdom;
> he knows where it can be found,
> For he looks throughout the whole earth
> and sees everything under the heavens.
> He decided how hard the winds should blow
> and how much rain should fall.
> He made the laws for the rain and
> laid out a path for the lightning.
> Then he saw wisdom and evaluated it.
> He set it in place and examined it thoroughly.
> And this is what he says to all humanity:
> 'The fear of the LORD is true wisdom;
> to forsake evil is real understanding.'"
> (Job 28:23–28 NLT)

---

[68] Job 8:5–6.

Job, unlike his friends, makes no pretense of being wise. What we learn from him here is well summed up by Socrates, whose friends insist he is a wise man. "If I am a wise man it is because I know I am not a wise man." Job expands that premise in clearly attributing wisdom to the Singular, Eternal, Preexisting, and Uncreated Being. It is he who not only created the heavens and the earth but remains their commander down to the last drop of rain, the velocity of the wind, and the route of lightning.[69]

In addition to determining and managing the elements, he also sets in place wisdom and leaves bickering philosophers and theologians the sum of it: "The fear of the LORD is true wisdom; to forsake evil is real understanding."

> Then the LORD answered Job
> out of the whirlwind, and said:
> "Who is this who darkens counsel
> by words without knowledge?
> Now prepare yourself like a man;
> I will question you, and you shall answer Me.
> Where were you when
> I laid the foundations of the earth?
> Tell Me, if you have understanding.
> Who determined its measurements? Surely you know!
> Or who stretched the line upon it?
> To what were its foundations fastened?
> Or who laid its cornerstone,
> When the morning stars sang together,
> And all the sons of God shouted for joy?
> Or who shut in the sea with doors,
> When it burst forth and issued from the womb;
> When I made the clouds its garment,
> And thick darkness its swaddling band;
> When I fixed My limit for it, And set bars and doors;

---

[69] Colossians 2:1–3—Jesus Christ, the eternal Son of God, as the source of "all the treasures of wisdom and knowledge."

When I said,`This far you may come, but no farther,
And here your proud waves must stop!'"
(Job 38:11 NKJV)

This is the ultimate, "Well, shut my mouth" of all literature. "Who is this who darkens counsel by words without knowledge?" The query is addressed to Job but applicable to his three friends that remain silent through the rest of the book of Job. Amid a recap of creation, the LORD lays down the ultimate challenge to all who would call into question his rights or his ways or his means—"Where were *you* when *I* laid down the foundations of the earth?"

"Who shut in the sea with doors,
When it burst forth and issued from the womb?"
(Job 38:8 NKJV)

"Can you draw out Leviathan with a hook,
Or snare his tongue with a line which you lower?
Can you put a reed through his nose,
Or pierce his jaw with a hook?
Will he make many supplications to you?
Will he speak softly to you?
Will he make a covenant with you?
Will you take him as a servant forever?
Will you play with him as with a bird,
Or will you leash him for your maidens?"
(Job 41:1–5 NKJV)

The LORD opens his verbal barrage upon Job with a debilitating query and two humbling follow-ups: "Where were you when I laid the foundations of the earth? Tell me if you have understanding; surely you know."[70]

In soaring, biting, sarcastic, in-your-face poetry, the LORD informs his intellectually disarmed audience of his masterpiece of architecture and

---

[70] Job 38:4–5.

engineering—the earth, the heavens, and especially the seas. In the forty-first chapter of the book, the LORD reminds Job that he not only created the seas but he remains the master of even its mightiest beast. He calls to mind the Leviathan (dreaded sea monster of ancient lore) and compares his domination of Leviathan to man's pulling in a fish or taming a pet.

> Then Job answered the LORD and said:
> "I know that You can do everything,
> And that no purpose of yours can be withheld from you.
> Therefore I abhor myself, and repent in dust
> and ashes." (Job 42:1–2, 6 NKJV)

Job's story ends with no further explanation of suffering than that it is ultimately the Sovereign LORD's business—and his alone.

True to his LORD-bestowed accolade as "a blameless and upright man, one who fears God and shuns evil," Job repents in dust and ashes. Satan, not heard from since chapter two, apparently has slinked away to plot a comeback elsewhere. The three friends are admonished by the LORD, ordered to sacrifice, repentance, and to an eat crow reconciliation with Job.

Job, apparently well cured of painful flesh and once again chummy with Mrs. Job, fathers a new family of seven boys and three girls, is restored to twofold wealth, and lives well over one hundred years.

YOU DIVIDED THE SEAS

> O God, how long will the adversary reproach?
> Will the enemy blaspheme Your name forever?
> Why do You withdraw Your hand, even Your right hand?
> Take it out of Your bosom and destroy them.
> For God is my King from of old,
> Working salvation in the midst of the earth.
> You divided the sea by Your strength;
> You broke the heads of the sea serpents in the waters.

> You broke the heads of Leviathan in pieces,
> And gave him as food
> to the people inhabiting the wilderness.
> You broke open the fountain and the flood;
> You dried up mighty rivers. (Psalm 74:10–15 NKJV)

Old Testament psalmists, just as Job and his friends, struggled with the problem of suffering. Why? How long? Usually they had a good idea "why." The disobedience and blatant insurrection of God's people had led to all manner of misery courtesy of natural disaster, civil unrest, foreign enemies, and more. How long the current withdrawal of God's protective and gracious hand would last was another matter.

The poet/songwriter of Psalm 74, appealing for relief, nails what Jesus Christ would describe as the best way for his disciples to open a prayer: "Our father in heaven, Hallowed [holy] be your name, your kingdom come, your will be done on earth as it is in heaven." He recognizes and praises the everlasting one, who is king, who is creator, whose will is sovereign and who must ultimately save, stretching forth once again his long arm of protection.[71]

> The young lions roar after their prey,
> And seek their food from God.
> When the sun rises, they gather together
> And lie down in their dens.
> Man goes out to his work
> And to his labor until the evening.
> O LORD, how manifold are Your works!
> In wisdom You have made them all.
> The earth is full of Your possessions—
> This great and wide sea,
> In which are innumerable teeming things,
> Living things both small and great.
> There the ships sail about;

---

[71] Matthew 6:9–10.

> There is that Leviathan
> Which You have made to play there.
> These all wait for You,
> That You may give them their food in due season.
> (Psalm 104:21–27 NKJV)

Here three of the more unpredictable products of creation, man, the lion, and that nasty monstrous leviathan of the sea all find rest, sustenance, and safety in the all-wise master builder of the heavens and the earth. Food from God, possessions from God, even rest and recreation—from God. It may be significant that in this Psalm the most violent and fearful of animals find security in the great provider. Yet for always reticent man, Jesus finds it prudent to add another petition to the prayer he taught his disciples—"Give us this day our daily bread."[72] Being content in the provision of each day will be an ongoing challenge for God's people.

MY SOUL THIRSTS FOR GOD

> [To the chief musician,
> a contemplation of the sons of Korah]
> As the deer pants for the water brooks,
> So pants my soul for You, O God.
> My soul thirsts for God, for the living God.
> When shall I come and appear before God?
> My tears have been my food day and night,
> While they continually say to me,
> "Where is your God?"
> When I remember these things,
> I pour out my soul within me.
> For I used to go with the multitude;
> I went with them to the house of God,
> With the voice of joy and praise,
> With a multitude that kept a pilgrim feast.
> Why are you cast down, O my soul?

---

[72] Matthew 6:11.

And why are you disquieted within me?
Hope in God, for I shall yet praise Him
For the help of His countenance.
O my God, my soul is cast down within me;
Therefore I will remember You
from the land of the Jordan,
And from the heights of Hermon, From the Hill Mizar.
Deep calls unto deep at the noise of Your waterfalls;
All Your waves and billows have gone over me.
(Psalm 42:1–7 NKJV)

Psalm 42 is a veritable amphibious roller coaster of emotion riding over, through, and under a brook, a river, waterfalls, waves, and billows.

The soul of its singer first bends reflectively, on joyous knees at the banks of a bubbling brook, panting for oneness with its creator. All the while its tears cry out, "Where is your God?" Soul returns to better days recalling the joy of ascending with other pilgrims to a feast at the house of God. Then it cascades downward, first talking to itself, then to God on matters of disquiet and of hope before it crashes crestfallen below a tidal wave of watery woe.

[A psalm of the sons of Korah]
How lovely is Your tabernacle, O LORD of hosts!
My soul longs, yes, even faints
For the courts of the LORD;
My heart and my flesh cry out for the living.
Blessed is the man whose strength is in You,
Whose heart is set on pilgrimage.
As they pass through the Valley of Baca,
They make it a spring;
The rain also covers it with pools.
They go from strength to strength;
Each one appears before God in Zion.
(Psalm 84:1–2, 5–7 NKJV)

The sons of Korah, descendants of the priestly tribe of Levi, reprise the subject of pilgrimage, this time triumphantly. "Blessed is the man whose strength is in you, whose heart is set on pilgrimage." The LORD's pilgrim reaches the Valley of Baca (weeping). He will neither turn back nor linger. His soul longs for that which is beyond—the courts of the LORD. He passes into, but then through, the vale of tears. He leaves behind, going strength to strength, a valley bubbling from below as a spring and sprinkled from above by heavenly rains.

LET THE SEAS ROAR

Praise the LORD!
Praise the LORD from the heavens;
Praise Him in the heights!
Praise Him, all His angels; Praise Him, all His hosts!
Praise Him, sun and moon;
Praise Him, all you stars of light!
Praise Him, you heavens of heavens,
And you waters above the heavens!
Let them praise the name of the LORD,
For He commanded and they were created.
He also established them forever and ever;
He made a decree which shall not pass away.
Praise the LORD from the earth,
You great sea creatures and all the depths;
Fire and hail, snow and clouds;
Stormy wind, fulfilling His word.
(Psalm 148:1–8 NKJV)

Fifty-nine percent of the 207 usages of the word *praise* occur in the Psalms. The word connotes something close to "boast." Here the songwriter rewinds back to creation capturing the products of that divine labor joining in glad adoration of their maker. Angels, heights, depths, sun, moon, heaven of heavens, the waters, and their inhabitants—all boast only of the I AM.

Finally, and fittingly, even surly fire, hail, snow, and clouds bow in obedience to him in fulfillment of his word.

Amid the very real perplexity of disorder in their own lives, the congregation revels in an underlying and overlaying truth—the LORD has got it all together, not just now but eternally. "He also established them forever and ever; He made a decree which shall not pass away."

> Sing to the LORD with the harp,
> With the harp and the sound of a psalm,
> With trumpets and the sound of a horn;
> Shout joyfully before the LORD, the King.
> Let the sea roar, and all its fullness,
> The world and those who dwell in it;
> Let the rivers clap their hands;
> Let the hills be joyful together before the LORD,
> For He is coming to judge the earth.
> With righteousness He shall judge the world,
> And the peoples with equity. (Psalm 98:5–9 NKJV)

After many decades, hearts still come alive with the opening of the 1965 movie *The Sound of Music*. From the opening scene, the viewer knows that the hills are alive with it, the sound of music, that is.

Long before the ecstatic line was fed to the movie's star, Julie Andrews, it was penned for worshiping congregations of ancient Israel. Not only are the hills "joyful together," but the rivers "clap their hands." Why all this exhilaration? Because the LORD hasn't forgotten his creation and never will. He is not only coming to judge the world and its peoples but to do so with "righteousness" and "equity."

> Then to Adam He said,
> "Because you have heeded the voice of your wife,
> and have eaten from the tree of which I commanded
> you, saying, 'You shall not eat of it':
> Cursed is the ground for your sake;

In toil you shall eat of it All the days of your life."
(Genesis 3:17 NKJV)

For we know that the whole creation groans
and labors with birth pangs together until now.
(Romans 8:22 NKJV)

Let the rivers clap their hands;
Let the hills be joyful together. (Psalm 98:8 NKJV)

The Old Testament poets in their joy before the LORD ascribed voice, just as jubilant as theirs, to rivers and hills. Yet in the midst of man's labor-intensive gardens, the thorns and thistles continued their relentless advance. If those rivers and hills were really singing, they were singing in a decisively minor key. Adam had been cursed for his rebellion. Innocent creation, just standing there minding its own business, took the death blow along with him.

Writers of the Bible were inspired to take pains predicting humanity's relief in the form of a second chance—a new birth in the form of a second Adam, a Savior. The apostle Paul, hundreds of years after David and Jeremiah, speaks of a do over for creation, as well. Its pregnancy has been long and agonizing— "until now." It is the "until now" to which all scripture after the fall speaks. And it is the stuff that can make even rivers clap their hands.

[A psalm of David]
Give unto the LORD, O you mighty ones,
Give unto the LORD glory and strength.
Give unto the LORD the glory due to His name;
Worship the LORD in the beauty of holiness.
The voice of the LORD is over the waters;
The God of glory thunders;
The LORD is over many waters.
The voice of the LORD is powerful;
The voice of the LORD is full of majesty.
(Psalm 29:1–4 NKJV)

King David, monarch and soldier, expanded his nation's borders and influence significantly, leaving Israel to his son, Solomon, as a stable and significant force in the always turbulent ancient Middle East. He never, however, lost sight of the real King. Here he poetically instructs those mightier than he, the "mighty ones" of heaven—the LORD's contingent of angels—to give credit where credit is alone due—the glory due his very name.

Give, give, give ... unto the LORD, unto the LORD, unto the LORD. Worship him in the "beauty of his holiness." For this is the God of awe— whose very voice thunders over the waters. The waterfall may thunder in power to the rocks below. Thrones may rise and fall. It is the LORD who made both and whose voice thunders from above. His voice is the voice full of unlimited majesty that speaks before, past, and above every his or her majesty who has ever come or whoever yet will be.

WE PAY FOR THE WATER WE DRINK

The LORD of hosts has sworn by Himself:
"Surely I will fill you with men, as with locusts,
And they shall lift up a shout against you."
He has made the earth by His power;
He has established the world by His wisdom,
And stretched out the heaven by His understanding.
When He utters His voice—
There is a multitude of waters in the heavens:
"He causes the vapors to ascend
from the ends of the earth;
He makes lightnings for the rain;
He brings the wind out of His treasuries."
Everyone is dull-hearted, without knowledge;
Every metalsmith is put to shame by the carved image;
For his molded image is falsehood,
And there is no breath in them.
They are futile, a work of errors;

> In the time of their punishment they shall
> perish. (Jeremiah 51:14–18 NKJV)

By the time of the prophet Jeremiah, David's once flourishing kingdom is in shambles. Powerful and brutal Babylon is about to ravage idolatrous Judah, the surviving bastion of ancient Israel. Jeremiah has exhausted himself megaphoning the LORD's warnings into deaf ears. He returns to the beginning—a marvelous earth created by God's voice, wisdom, and power.

All the life-giving waters of heaven and earth are propelled to their appointed destinations by him. Yet you dull-hearted and dim-witted choose the metal smith's sculpted carved image. Be clear on this. They are on their way out. "In the time of their punishment they shall perish."

> How lonely sits the city That was full of people!
> How like a widow is she,
> Who was great among the nations!
> The princess among the provinces Has become a slave!
> She weeps bitterly in the night,
> Her tears are on her cheeks;
> Among all her lovers She has none to comfort her.
> All her friends have dealt treacherously with her;
> They have become her enemies.
> (Lamentations 1:1–2 NKJV)

> The steadfast love of the LORD never ceases;
> his mercies never come to an end.
> (Lamentations 3:22 ESV)

> We pay for the water we drink,
> And our wood comes at a price (NKJV).

Jeremiah is sometimes called the "weeping prophet" for good reason. He cries a lot. He agonizes over the people he loves who will not listen to the only being in the universe who could and does love them despite their insolence. He weeps on behalf of the city he treasures, now decimated by the treacherous but long-predicted Babylonians.

The prophet's profusion of tears permeate the entire book of Lamentations—appropriately named—a lament over Jerusalem, a city intended to be a princess among cities, now a devastated and abandoned widow. Only in the chapter three center of Lamentations does Jeremiah reveal his personal abiding core center, a LORD who never abandons, "whose mercies never come to an end."

COME TO THE WATERS

Ho, every one who thirsts, come to the waters;
and he who has no money, come, buy and eat!
Come, buy wine and milk without money
and without price. (Isaiah 55:1 ESV)

Isaiah's warnings to a united Israel were about as successful as most of the other prophets. The LORD God, slow to anger and abounding in steadfast love, eventually allowed Assyrians, predecessors to the Babylonians, to conquer the tribes of Israel to the north.

Like Jeremiah, Isaiah took time from his busy schedule of prophetic warning to extol the generosity of a LORD perfectly willing to feed and quench those left around who might be interested in restoring or entering a true covenant relationship with him.

In a message to the poor in spirit and flesh, the prophet offers water, milk, even wine—without price. No free lunch? Amazing grace, undeserved mercy for the thirsty and hungry, is thematic to the entire Bible. It will capture the essence of the kingdom of God itself.

God blesses those who are poor and realize their need
for him, for the Kingdom of Heaven is theirs.
(Matthew 5:3 (NLT)

> **Blessed are those who hunger and thirst for righteousness,
> for they shall be filled. (Matthew 5:6 NKJV)**[73]

> [A psalm of David when
> he was in the wilderness of Judah]
> O God, You are my God; Early will I seek You;
> My soul thirsts for You; My flesh longs for You
> In a dry and thirsty land Where there is no water.
> So I have looked for You in the sanctuary,
> To see Your power and Your glory.
> Because Your loving kindness is better than life,
> My lips shall praise You.
> Thus I will bless You while I live;
> I will lift up my hands in Your name.
> (Psalm 63:1–4 NKJV)

It is absolutely fitting that thirst should be a recurring theme for poets and prophets. They do not reside in the land of the Nile, the Tigris, or the Euphrates. Theirs is a dry domain where any brook or oasis is welcome.

King David zeroes directly to God's life-giving water. He knows the wilderness of the soul. He knows, as well, the oasis that is God himself. David's very being—soul and flesh—pants in the desert for the spring of the LORD.

This is a poem of verbs, of a king diligently seeking to bow before his own monarch. That very entity which is David is dry and thirsty; his flesh and soul long for God's sanctuary. The soul that knows its need cannot and will not lay back waiting for the water to come to him. David seeks, and he seeks "early." He looks into his monarch's sanctuary. He is rewarded with 20/20 vision—the power and glory of the LORD whose loving kindness is better than life. David's thirsty lips respond with praise and blessings. His hands rise in worship.

---

[73] From the Sermon on the Mount of Jesus, Matthew chapters 5–7.

Seek the LORD while He may be found,
Call upon Him while He is near.
Let the wicked forsake his way,
And the unrighteous man his thoughts;
Let him return to the LORD,
And He will have mercy on him;
And to our God, For He will abundantly pardon.
"For My thoughts are not your thoughts,
Nor are your ways My ways," says the LORD.
"For as the heavens are higher than the earth,
So are My ways higher than your ways,
And My thoughts than your thoughts.
For as the rain comes down, and the snow from
heaven, And do not return there,
But water the earth, And make it bring forth and bud,
That it may give seed to the sower and bread to the eater,
So shall My word be that goes forth from My mouth;
It shall not return to Me void,
But it shall accomplish what I please,
And it shall prosper in the thing for which I sent it."
(Isaiah 55:6–11 NKJV)

Isaiah cries out to the wicked and unrighteous of way and thought, "Seek the LORD," "Return to the LORD." He will have mercy and abundantly pardon. His thoughts, after all, are no more comparable to man's than the height of earth compares to that of the heavens. And one way or another, he will have his way. Like the rain and snow that feed the waters and prosper the labor of the sower, so his word will not return to him empty. "It shall accomplish what I please."

VANITY OF VANITIES

The words of the Preacher,
the son of David, king in Jerusalem.
"Vanity of vanities," says the Preacher;
"Vanity of vanities, all is vanity."

What profit has a man from all his labor
In which he toils under the sun?
One generation passes away,
and another generation comes;
But the earth abides forever.
The sun also rises, and the sun goes down,
And hastens to the place where it arose.
The wind goes toward the south,
And turns around to the north;
The wind whirls about continually,
And comes again on its circuit.
All the rivers run into the sea, Yet the sea is not full;
To the place from which the rivers come,
There they return again.
(Ecclesiastes 1:1–7 NKJV)

The preacher (King Solomon) adds his take on the subject of waters spilling downward, this time into the sea. His concern, however, is not a call to repentance but to a consideration of just whether there is anything in life that is not in its beginning and end mere vanity. He explores pleasure, labor, and even wisdom along with other compulsions of the human soul. He concludes that all are as vain and tedious as the winds and waters, which inevitably return to whence they began.

So what has meaning? He concludes his twelve-chapter treatise as follows: "Of making many books there is no end, and much study is wearisome to the flesh. Let us hear the conclusion of the whole matter: Fear God and keep His commandments. For this is man's all. For God will bring every work into judgment, including every secret thing, whether good or evil."[74]

BROKEN CISTERNS

"Therefore I will yet bring charges against you,"
says the LORD,

---

[74] Ecclesiastes 12:12–14.

"And against your children's children I will bring charges.
For pass beyond the coasts of Cyprus and see,
Send to Kedar and consider diligently,
And see if there has been such a thing.
Has a nation changed its gods, Which are not gods?
But My people have changed their Glory
For what does not profit.
Be astonished, O heavens, at this, And be horribly afraid;
Be very desolate," says the LORD.
"For My people have committed two evils:
They have forsaken Me, the fountain of living waters,
And hewn themselves cisterns—
broken cisterns that can hold no water."
(Jeremiah 2:9–13 NKJV)

The LORD, slow to anger and abounding in steadfast love, unleashes his wrath neither with haste nor caprice. On occasion he presents his case judicially as a divine prosecutor enumerating charges against his covenant-crashing people.

Here are the liberally paraphrased offenses with a blistering preface and postscript, as transcribed by court reporter Jeremiah: You beat all! Check it out! Is there any other nation known to have switched gods? They, at least, remained loyal to their impotent wood and iron. But you …! You have swapped God-given glory for that which has no value or even reality. The very heavens are astonished. You, the LORD's obstinate ingrates, have forsaken the sparkling stream of eternal "living waters" for leaky cisterns of your own making. Be horribly afraid.

HE WATERS THE HILLS

Bless the LORD, O my soul! O LORD my God,
You are very great:
You are clothed with honor and majesty,
He sends the springs into the valleys,

They flow among the hills.
They give drink to every beast of the field;
The wild donkeys quench their thirst.
By them the birds of the heavens have their home;
They sing among the branches.
He waters the hills from His upper chambers;
The earth is satisfied with the fruit of Your works.
He causes the grass to grow for the cattle,
And vegetation for the service of man,
That he may bring forth food from the earth.
(Psalm 104:1 NKJV)

This faithful covenant man of the LORD finds his God not in the temporary, transitory carvings and moldings of artists but in the Singular, Eternal, Preexisting, and Uncreated Being who defies material depiction. It is not in togas or hides of bulls that this God is clothed. He is, instead and exclusively, arrayed beyond human comprehension in "honor and majesty."

The psalmist's thirst is quenched from no broken man-made container but from unlimited and unrestrained springs of eternal waters sufficient to satisfy man and beast and to render the birds of the trees helpless but to join his song of praise.

THE WELLSPRING OF WISDOM

Wisdom calls aloud outside;
She raises her voice in the open squares.
So that you incline your ear to wisdom,
And apply your heart to understanding;
Yes, if you cry out for discernment,
And lift up your voice for understanding,
If you seek her as silver,
And search for her as for hidden treasures;
Then you will understand the fear of the LORD,
And find the knowledge of God.

> For the LORD gives wisdom;
> From His mouth come knowledge and understanding;
> He stores up sound wisdom for the upright;
> He is a shield to those who walk uprightly;
> He guards the paths of justice,
> And preserves the way of His saints.
> Then you will understand righteousness and justice, Equity
> and every good path. (Proverbs 1:1, 2:2–9 NKJV)

King Solomon in Proverbs, a book of wisdom replete with common-sense sayings, calls his son to seek wisdom—a gift of God reflective of his very essence. "She" is available to the young man who will "incline" his ear, "apply his heart," "lift up his voice," and "seek her" as diligently as he would search out hidden treasures.

She is a beautiful and bounteous lady. It is she who ushers the young man into a world of knowledge and understanding from which he will in turn store sound wisdom for the upright, shield those who walk uprightly, and guard their paths in justice, preserving their righteous ways.

Wisdom calls loudly over the tumult of the open squares. Other voices will coo and shriek in competition. Hers comes with a guarantee. If, my son, you listen and seek earnestly you will approach the very heart of the LORD, understanding "righteousness, justice, equity and every good path."

> Listen to your father who begot you,
> And do not despise your mother when she is old.
> Buy the truth, and do not sell it,
> Also wisdom and instruction and understanding.
> The father of the righteous will greatly rejoice,
> And he who begets a wise child will delight in him.
> Let your father and your mother be glad,
> And let her who bore you rejoice.
> My son, give me your heart,
> And let your eyes observe my ways.
> For a harlot is a deep pit,

And a seductress is a narrow well.
(Proverbs 22:23–27 NKJV)

The LORD held such high regard for parenthood that He included, among His Ten Commandments, "Honor your father and mother that your days may be long upon the land which the LORD your God is giving you."[75] Here Wisdom urges love and respect of parents and calls for a life that will move them to delight.

Wisdom is aware of rivals for a young man's affection and warns of "the other woman," the one at the "narrow well."

Counsel in the heart of man is like deep water,
But a man of understanding will draw it out.
(Proverbs 20:5 NKJV)

The words of a man's mouth are deep waters;
The wellspring of wisdom is a flowing brook.
(Proverbs 18:4 NKJV)

The law of the wise is a fountain of life,
To turn one away from the snares of death.
(Proverbs 13:14 NKJV)

Proverbs often appear in couplet form. In these three gems of universal and timeless advice, the young man is called to Lady Wisdom through the simile and metaphor of water.

Counsel from the heart of man may be either beneficial or injurious. Its essence is not generally to be seen at a glance. It must be drawn out by the "man of understanding," as must be the best and most refreshing waters of a deep well. It must be searched for consciously and lifted in the trustworthy dipper of wisdom.

---

[75] Exodus 20:12.

Similarly the words of any man's mouth originate in his spiritual depths. The well of his true being is still and deep and unseen. But from the man of wisdom will outflow a bubbling spring of wisdom parenting a flowing brook.

Just as wells from deep water and flowing brooks birth and then nurture life, so turning from the instruction of the LORD, the law of the wise, is a side trip of no return into the snares of death.

> **The generous soul will be made rich,**
> **And he who waters will also be watered**
> **himself. (Proverbs 11:25 NKJV)**

> **If your enemy is hungry, give him bread to eat;**
> **And if he is thirsty, give him water to drink**
> **For so you will heap coals of fire on his head,**
> **And the LORD will reward you.**
> **(Proverbs 25:21–22 NKJV)**

King Solomon returns to the well of highest wisdom, calling his son to enrich his own soul through watering the souls of others. He raises the bar of kindness to levels unheard of in the ancient world. This includes your enemies, son. If he is hungry, feed him. If he is thirsty, give him water.

A thousand years later, Jesus will amplify the already staggering instruction. "You have heard that it was said, 'You shall love your neighbor and hate your enemy' But I say to you, love your enemies, bless those who curse you, do good to those who hate you, and pray for those who spitefully use you and persecute you, that you may be sons of your Father in heaven; for he makes his sun rise on the evil and on the good, and sends rain on the just and on the unjust."[76]

> **Drink water from your own cistern,**
> **And running water from your own well.**
> **Should your fountains be dispersed abroad,**

---

[76] Matthew 5:43–45.

Streams of water in the streets?
Let them be only your own,
And not for strangers with you.
Let your fountain be blessed,
And rejoice with the wife of your youth.
As a loving deer and a graceful doe,
Let her breasts satisfy you at all times;
And always be enraptured with her love.
(Proverbs 5:15–19 NKJV)

The Bible neither shies from controversial topics nor blushes in them. Consider this proverbial entry which has nothing to do with wells, cisterns, and fountains and everything to do with, well …

We learn that the "fountain" is once again a metaphor. It identifies what more delicately falls into the domain of the "birds and bees." When all is said, done, and finalized in one hundred words or less, Solomon makes an unequivocal stand for the sanctity of marriage, complete with a resounding endorsement of wildly joyful conjugality within its borders. The unity of one man with one woman established by none other than the LORD back in the Garden of Eden will be wholeheartedly seconded by the Son of God, Jesus Christ in these words:

"And he answered and said to them, 'Have you not read that he who made them at the beginning made them male and female', and said, "For this reason a man shall leave his father and mother and be joined to his wife, and the two shall become one flesh?" So then, they are no longer two but one flesh. Therefore what God has joined together, let not man separate."[77]

THE WATERS WOULD HAVE OVERWHELMED US

[A Song of Ascents. Of David]
"If it had not been the LORD who was on our side,"

---

[77] Matthew19:4–6.

Let Israel now say—
"If it had not been the LORD who was on our side,
When men rose up against us,
Then they would have swallowed us alive,
When their wrath was kindled against us;
Then the waters would have overwhelmed us,
The stream would have gone over our soul;
Then the swollen waters Would have gone
over our soul." (Psalm 124:1 NKJV)

There is a river whose streams make glad the city of God,
the holy place where the Most High dwells.
(Psalm 46:4 NIV)

King David, a seasoned warrior, knew what it was to face an overwhelming foe. It was akin to withstanding a raging flash flood in the desert. Hopeless. Had it "not been the LORD who was on our side ... we would have been swallowed alive." Hopeless. David and those marching upward to Zion (Jerusalem) rejoiced over a river of hope and victory that was not a river at all but the very LORD God who alone had saved them and was ready and waiting to do so again.

PART IV

Slavery to Salvation

Moses

> Then the LORD said to him [Abraham],
> "Know for certain that your descendants
> will be strangers in a country not their own,
> and they will be enslaved and
> mistreated four hundred years.
> But I will punish the nation they serve as slaves,
> and afterward they will come out with great
> possessions." (Genesis 15:13–14 NIV)

With the LORD it always seems to come back to "covenant." And here's where it all started. He has assured Abraham of a multitude of descendants, regardless of his wife's aged and barren womb. He has further promised Abraham a specific geographic site for the abundant national population yet to come. The LORD never reneges on a bargain.

But equally he wants it known "for certain" that Abraham's extended family will mess up the deal as surely as his two earliest ancestors paired up to dismantle paradise. Abe is not to deceive himself into believing that only rose gardens lie ahead. That has been tried and found wanting. "Know for certain ..." (1) your descendants will be estranged in someone else's land, (2) the "someone elses" are nasty to the utmost.

The Holy Bible is filled with warning, reproof, and correction often accompanied by reassuring words such as "but I" or "but God" or "but the LORD." No exception here in the very place where course direction and course correction begin. "But I" will punish your enemies, and you will come out of four hundred years of abuse with "great possessions."

> But as the time of the promise drew near,
> which God had granted to Abraham,
> the people increased and multiplied in Egypt
> until there arose over Egypt
> another king who did not know Joseph.
> He dealt shrewdly with our race
> and forced our fathers to expose their infants,
> so that they would not be kept alive.
> At this time Moses was born;
> and he was beautiful in God's sight.
> And he was brought up for three months
> in his father's house,
> and when he was exposed,
> Pharaoh's daughter adopted him
> and brought him up as her own son.
> And Moses was instructed
> in all the wisdom of the Egyptians,
> and he was mighty in his words and deeds.
> (Acts 7:17–22 ESV)

These words are spoken by the first person to die for the faith that came to be called Christianity. His name is Stephen. Here he is beginning, for the benefit of those about to stone him to death, an account of the LORD God's plan of salvation—a plan to be built around a flawless sacrifice for sin and failure. This sacrifice will come courtesy of the murder of all ages and be far more shocking than even that of Stephen—the death of the LORD God's own son. As if to highlight the need for someone to finally halt an endless chronology of human misery and demise, the entire Old Testament will be stained profusely with blood, as will the mighty Nile River and its less than invincible desert kingdom of Egypt.

> **In the course of those many days the king of Egypt died.**
> **And the people of Israel groaned under their bondage,**
> **and cried out for help,**
> **and their cry under bondage came up to God.**
> **And God heard their groaning,**
> **and God remembered his covenant**
> **with Abraham, with Isaac, and with Jacob.**
> **And God saw the people of Israel,**
> **and God knew their condition. (Exodus 2:23–25 RSV)**

Moses, through a divine act of intervention during a time of royally decreed infanticide, was, ironically, brought to be raised in the palace of the pharaoh, himself. We know nothing of Moses' childhood nor of his first forty years other than his being a fine specimen of a human being, "mighty in words and deeds" and "instructed in all the wisdom of the Egyptians"—no minor doctorate as history and archaeology have demonstrated.

What is always more important in the Bible narrative is not what a man or men and women are doing or planning but what the LORD God is doing and what plans he has made. What the people are doing is groaning and crying out under the pressing weight of slavery. It's help they want. We have no idea whose aid they are soliciting. Probably anyone who might listen.

It's the Singular, Eternal, Preexisting, and Uncreated Being who hears. He sees, as well. He sees his people. He remembers, as well. He remembers his covenant. And as can be expected of any omniscient being, he "knew their condition."

> **When Pharaoh heard of it, he sought to kill Moses.**
> **But Moses fled from Pharaoh**
> **and stayed in the land of Midian.**
> **And he sat down by a well.**

Now the priest of Midian had seven daughters,
and they came and drew water
and filled the troughs to water their father's flock.
The shepherds came and drove them away,
but Moses stood up and saved them,
and watered their flock.
When they came home to their father Reuel, he said,
"How is it that you have come home so soon today?"
They said, "An Egyptian delivered us
out of the hand of the shepherds
and even drew water for us and watered the
flock." (Exodus 2:15–19 ESV)

What Pharaoh heard about was murder. Moses, like God, had looked upon the burdens being borne by the Hebrews. Apparently convinced he could *play* God better than God could *be* God, he rubbed out an Egyptian who was in the act of pummeling one of the Hebrew slaves. Pharaoh responded, ordering the death of Moses, sending him into rapid and distant retreat.[78] Once again a hero of the people ends up at a local watering hole populated by young maidens. Moses emerges hero of the day and begins his second forty years far from his royal avenger, safe in the land of Midian and, as may be expected, married to one of the cooing young ladies.

Forty years later, in the desert near Mount Sinai,
an angel appeared to Moses
in the flame of a burning bush.
When Moses saw it, he was amazed at the sight.
As he went to take a closer look,
the voice of the LORD called out to him,
"I am the God of your ancestors—
the God of Abraham, Isaac, and Jacob."
Moses shook with terror and did not dare to look.
Then the LORD said to him, "Take off your sandals,
for you are standing on holy ground.

---

[78] Exodus 2:11–14.

I have certainly seen the oppression of my people in Egypt.
I have heard their groans and
have come down to rescue them.
Now go, for I am sending you back to Egypt."
(Acts 7:30–34 NLT)

Centuries had passed since the last close encounter with the Singular, Eternal, Preexisting, and Uncreated Being who desires a covenant relationship with his people. His dramatic impact is not to be minimized. Moses, recording the incident himself, tells us he was scared stiff.

What the LORD first establishes is who is boss. Moses, when you are in my company, your very feet stand on holy ground. Take off your shoes in my house!

As if Moses did not already have a day for the ages, he is further informed that the LORD has remembered his covenant. "I have heard their groans and have come down to rescue them." Great news. "Now go, for I am sending you back to Egypt." Bad news. There must be a misprint here. Moses will plead ineptitude on the basis of poor speech, inferiority, bad odds—everything short of insanity. No avail. There *will be* a rescue, a salvation, an intervention, and the LORD and Moses will be in it together.[79]

But Moses protested,
"If I go to the people of Israel and tell them,
'The God of your ancestors has sent me to you,'
they will ask me, 'What is his name?'
Then what should I tell them?"
God replied to Moses, "I AM WHO I AM.
Say this to the people of Israel:
'I AM has sent me to you.'"
God also said to Moses, "Say this to the people of Israel:
'Yahweh, the God of your ancestors—
the God of Abraham, the God of Isaac, and

---

[79] Exodus 3:11–4:17.

> the God of Jacob—has sent me to you.'
> This is my eternal name,
> my name to remember for all generations."
> (Exodus 3:13–15 NLT)

After establishing who is boss, the LORD officially hangs his shingle on the law office door. "My name is I AM WHO I AM." You can't beat that for Singular, Eternal, Preexisting, and Uncreated Being: omnipotent, omniscient, and omnipresent. Moses' last appeal for draft exemption had been to assert that he had no way of identifying the true God who was about to step again into history. Here's what you tell them, Moses. Tell them my name is I AM. And tell them not to forget it.

> But the LORD said to Moses,
> "Now you shall see what I will do to Pharaoh;
> for with a strong hand he will send them out,
> and with a strong hand he will drive them out of his land."
> God spoke to Moses and said to him, "I am the LORD.
> I appeared to Abraham, to Isaac,
> and to Jacob, as God Almighty,
> but by my name the LORD
> I did not make myself known to them.
> I also established my covenant with them
> to give them the land of Canaan,
> the land in which they lived as sojourners."
> (Exodus 6:1–4 ESV)

Hebrew biblical writing is rich in repetition. Here the LORD reiterates his name, his covenant, and his strategy. His strategy is to bring Abraham's now numerous covenantal descendants to the Promised Land to occupy it for the glory of his name. His tactics will be replete with astonishing miracles.

What will be done to Pharaoh by the LORD's "strong hand" will cause Egypt's king, himself, to *demand* that the Hebrew slaves leave Egypt. It will cause the Nile to run red and cause a sea to wall up in dutiful obedience to its creator. It will cause a lightweight Middle East stream called the Jordan to be the here, now, and endless symbol of rescue. And in the end, his people will forever have cause to remember their deliverance and to remember the name of the LORD.

> **Now Moses was eighty years old,**
> **and Aaron eighty-three years old,**
> **when they spoke to Pharaoh.**
> **Then the LORD said to Moses and Aaron,**
> **"When Pharaoh says to you,**
> **'Prove yourselves by working a miracle,'**
> **then you shall say to Aaron,**
> **'Take your staff and cast it down before Pharaoh,**
> **that it may become a serpent.'"** (Exodus 7:7–9 ESV)

It's time to teach Pharaoh a thing or ten by way of signs and wonders. For the task, the LORD pairs up Moses with his older brother, Aaron. In the case of these two, "old" is a relative term. Most men their age were dead.[80] Moses is about to begin his third and final set of forty years, the first having been spent in the palace of the king, the second in the wilderness of Midian.

Aaron, the more gifted speaker of the two, and his kid brother are given instructions on wowing the master of the Nile and greater metropolitan Egypt. There is going to be a showdown between pharaoh's magicians and sorcerers and the LORD. Magic wands versus a divinely charged staff? Who of the mortal "I wasn't always and may not be tomorrow" bunch mixes it up with the I Am, the Singular, Eternal, Preexisting, and Uncreated Being? *You* do if your boss is a king. Let the games begin!

> **So Moses and Aaron went to Pharaoh**
> **and did just as the LORD commanded.**
> **Aaron cast down his staff**
> **before Pharaoh and his servants,**
> **and it became a serpent.**

---

[80] This witticism belongs to the late New York Yankee manager, Casey Stengel speaking of himself in his seventies.

> Then Pharaoh summoned the wise men and the sorcerers,
> and they, the magicians of Egypt,
> also did the same by their secret arts.
> For each man cast down his staff,
> and they became serpents.
> But Aaron's staff swallowed up their staffs.
> (Exodus 7:10–12 ESV)

The Bible hasn't had much to say about reptiles since the deceiving one in Genesis slunk out of the garden he had so ably helped dishevel. Aaron throws down the gauntlet in the form of a staff, and it becomes a serpent. Presto, chango. Amazingly not one, but *every* one of the wise men, sorcerers, and magicians casts down his staff, matching the challenge in multiple manifestations of serpents. Prestidigitation supreme? Or able assistance from Satan, Job's old foe, well proven in the arts of the supernatural when permitted the opportunity?

In any case, this initial victory in a preliminary bout is soon reversed. The I Am's serpent turns out not to be impressed and devours the contenders. Not fair? Nobody said all this was going to be Marquis of Queensbury.[81]

> Then the LORD said to Moses,
> "Pharaoh's heart is hardened;
> he refuses to let the people go.
> Go to Pharaoh in the morning,
> as he is going out to the water.
> Stand on the bank of the Nile to meet him,
> and take in your hand the staff that turned into a serpent.
> And you shall say to him,
> 'The LORD, the God of the Hebrews,
> sent me to you, saying,
> Let my people go, that
> they may serve me in the wilderness.'

---

[81] Marquis of Queensberry rules, mid-nineteenth century, civilized boxing to a great extent and are centered around predictability and fair play in the sport.

> But so far, you have not obeyed."
> Thus says the LORD,
> "By this you shall know that I am the LORD:
> behold, with the staff that is in my hand
> I will strike the water that is in the Nile,
> and it shall turn into blood.
> The fish in the Nile shall die, and the Nile will stink,
> and the Egyptians will grow weary
> of drinking water from the Nile." (Exodus 7:14–18 ESV)

Moses shows up as uninvited guest and trespasser on the royal beach. He is armed with the staff that morphed into a serpent. Moses reminds the king of why he has returned:

1. The LORD has sent me.
2. He is displeased with your refusal to let his people go.
3. He plans to considerably pollute your beloved river.
4. All this is that you shall know "I am the LORD".

Point four of the pre-disaster announcement quite well capsualizes the LORD's recurring rationality for any and all of his corrective and disciplinary actions with both friend and foe: "that they shall know that I am the LORD."

> But the magicians of Egypt did the same
> [turned the river to blood]
> by their secret arts.
> So Pharaoh's heart remained hardened,
> and he would not listen to them, as the LORD had said.
> Pharaoh turned and went into his house,
> and he did not take even this to heart.
> And all the Egyptians dug
> along the Nile for water to drink,
> for they could not drink the water of the Nile.
> Seven full days passed after the LORD
> had struck the Nile. (Exodus 7:22–25 ESV)

Pharaoh, buoyed by his guys' ability to match marvels with Moses, walks out on the parlay. At worst it's a tie ball game. At best, maybe these Hebrew nuisances have had enough. Hardened of heart, he has no interest or necessity to negotiate with the LORD, let alone to acquiesce to him. In an early version of "let them eat cake,"[82] he spins a 180 and returns to the palace. There he spends seven days apparently drinking and bathing in stored clean water.

Down by the riverside, the reality is far different. Virtually everyone, "all the Egyptians," has become a well digger. Maybe it's not a tie ball game, after all.

> **So Aaron stretched out his hand over the waters of Egypt,**
> **and the frogs came up and covered the land of Egypt.**
> **But the magicians did the same by their secret arts**
> **and made frogs come up on the land of Egypt.**
> **Then Pharaoh called Moses and Aaron and said,**
> **"Plead with the LORD to take away**
> **the frogs from me and from my people,**
> **and I will let the people go to sacrifice to the**
> **LORD." (Exodus 8:6–8 ESV)**

If pharaoh had seen Moses and Aaron as pests, it was only to set the stage for several object lessons in the reality of pests. The next challenge was to replicate frogs in multitudes over the land. The magicians again were up to the task. Yet apparently more frogs represented a hollow victory. Even Pharaoh pleads "uncle." But there's more. If you will rid us of the amphibious assaulters, "I will let the people go out to sacrifice to their LORD."

No sooner said than done. On request from Moses, the LORD initiates frog demolition. The carcasses piled high "and the land stank."[83] The king plugged his nose and again walked out of the peace conference. Exit the overmatched magicians in the coming shows of power, except to urge

---

[82] Attributed to Marie Antoinette, wife of French King Louis XIV, on hearing of the starvation of the peasants.

[83] Exodus 8:14.

Pharaoh to yield for the good of the nation. This, after all, they say, is "the finger of God." [84] Gnats, flies, plagues, boils, and more are yet to come. And just in case the LORD's partisanship was not crystal clear, the Hebrews are exempted from the attacks.

> And the LORD gave the people favor
> in the sight of the Egyptians.
> Moreover, the man Moses
> was very great in the land of Egypt,
> in the sight of Pharaoh's servants
> and in the sight of the people.
> So Moses said, "Thus says the LORD:
> 'About midnight I will go out in the midst of Egypt,
> and every firstborn in the land of Egypt shall die,
> from the firstborn of Pharaoh who sits on his throne,
> even to the firstborn of the slave girl who is behind
> the handmill, and all the firstborn of the cattle.
> There shall be a great cry
> throughout all the land of Egypt,
> such as there has never been,
> nor ever will be again.'" (Exodus 11:3–6 ESV)

It's quite an understatement to say that the LORD gave the people "favor in the sight of the Egyptians"—considering their exemption from the misery of plague after plague. But it happened. And there was more to come. Not only did the Hebrew slaves exit Egypt after the final show of divine power; they left carrying treasures of Egyptian riches with them.[85]

Here and later, again and again in the history of the Jewish people, the LORD raises a leader, a savior, who by his hand rescues his unlikely and undeserving people from the formidable teeth of despair.

---

[84] Exodus 8:19.
[85] Exodus 12:35.

The hard-hearted Pharaoh has incurred the wrath of the LORD God, never an advisable endeavor. In response, the LORD announces his plan. Every firstborn, including cattle, will die this very night. The agony will be such as never has been before or after.

There will be one and only one notable exception. The LORD's people will be untouched.

> **"For I will pass through the land of Egypt that night,**
> **and I will strike all the firstborn in the land of Egypt,**
> **both man and beast;**
> **and on all the gods of Egypt I will execute judgments:**
> **I am the LORD.**
> **The blood shall be a sign for you,**
> **on the houses where you are.**
> **And when I see the blood, I will pass over you,**
> **and no plague will befall you to destroy you,**
> **when I strike the land of Egypt."**
> **(Exodus 12:12–13 ESV)**

The LORD had opened his demonstration of majesty and sovereignty by choking the mighty Nile in blood. With his tenth and last plague, on the night of Hebrew deliverance from the yoke of slavery, blood once again would flow in profusion. This time from the slit necks of innocent lambs. Never did the LORD "pass *through*" a people with such ferocity of judgment. Never did he "pass *over*" a people with such wealth of mercy. From this time forth, the sacrificial shedding of blameless blood would symbolize a divine amazing grace over people in bondage to sin and repression.

> **The LORD said to Moses and Aaron**
> **in the land of Egypt …**
> **"Tell all the congregation of Israel**
> **that on the tenth day of this month**
> **every man shall take a lamb**
> **according to their fathers' houses,**
> **a lamb for a household.**

> And if the household is too small for a lamb,
> then he and his nearest neighbor
> shall take according to the number of persons;
> according to what each can eat
> you shall make your count for the lamb.
> Your lamb shall be without blemish, a male a year old.
> You may take it from the sheep or from the goats,
> and you shall keep it
> until the fourteenth day of this month,
> when the whole assembly of the congregation of Israel
> shall kill their lambs at twilight."
> (Exodus 12:1, 3–6 ESV)

Hebrew population, as promised to Abraham and his family, had become as numerous as the "stars of heaven and as the sand which is on the seashore."[86] To what avail? They not only have no promised land but no freedom. Change is in the desert winds, however. That change will be marked by a festival to be observed through Jewish history to come. It will be called "Passover."

The night of deliverance will be highlighted by a feast. Its main course will be the body of an innocent lamb. Such startling cost could not go unnoticed by the ancient Jews. Each family will need to terminate the life of its prime male lamb—the unblemished one, the yearling. In his prime he must die—that they may live.

Nor should the intensity of this sacrifice go unnoticed by any modern reader who has snuggled a warm, newborn puppy—the pick of the litter! How devastating for a family to be told after one year of mutual companionship that the joyous, vibrant, romping, innocent, delightful, beloved free spirit has four days to live. In his prime he must die—that the family may live.

> For the life of the body is in its blood.
> I have given you the blood on the altar to purify you,
> making you right with the LORD.

---

[86] Genesis 22:17.

> ### It is the blood, given in exchange for a life,
> ### that makes purification possible. (Leviticus 17:11 (NLT)

Altars weren't novelties at the time of Moses. Pagans sacrificed animals out of fear and self-interest. Noah, Abraham, Isaac, and Jacob had sacrificed voluntarily from reverence and thanksgiving. Now at Passover, blood sacrifice was instituted as a present sign and a future remembrance and celebration of the LORD God's deliverance of his people from bondage.

Once the Hebrews were free of Egypt, the LORD God would mandate a variety of animal sacrifice ceremonies in addition to the yearly Passover observance. He not only could "stand the sight of blood" but demanded the sight of blood. "It is the blood, given in exchange for a life that makes purification possible." It is innocent blood that enables humans to be "right with the LORD." Out of death emerges life.

> ### For the life of the body is in its blood.
> ### I have given you the blood on the altar to purify you,
> ### making you right with the LORD.
> ### It is the blood, given in exchange for a life,
> ### that makes purification possible.
> ### (Leviticus 17:11 NLT)

Ninety two percent of plasma, blood's liquid component, is water. You can't have one without the other. They comingle. As surely as the LORD God drenched Pharaoh's Nile with blood, so the pages of scripture are saturated with the merging of blood and water. As life-giving water soaks the Bible's first and last chapters, so its chemical cousin, blood—in which life itself resides—watermarks itself as the Holy Book's theme and center. Its climax and resolution will come in the divinely human sacrifice of the blood of God's only son, Jesus Christ.

In the meantime, hundreds of thousands of lambs, bulls, goats, and pigeons were to be slain, in shaky compliance with a large body of ceremonial law intended to reconcile God and man. Why shaky?" Scripture is laden with examples of inferior product, grade B and downward animals, being offered as "gratitude" toward the creator, rescuer, and sustainer.

King David records in Psalm 51 that sacrifice is merely symbolic of what God really wants from his people—the sacrifice of a "broken spirit, a broken and a contrite heart." It is that which he will "not despise." Can anyone deliver on such a promise? The remainder of the Bible will point toward, at, or back at just such a one.

> **When Pharaoh let the people go,**
> **God did not lead them by way**
> **of the land of the Philistines,**
> **although that was near.**
> **For God said, "Lest the people change their minds**
> **when they see war and return to Egypt."**
> **But God led the people around by the way of**
> **the wilderness toward the Red Sea.**
> **And the people of Israel went up out of the land of Egypt**
> **equipped for battle. (Exodus 13:17–18 ESV)**

All happened as predicted. It's always the case when the LORD does the predicting. Death "passed through." Egypt lay in devastation, her firstborn, man and beast, extinguished in a night of divine retribution. Pharaoh finally relented, grief stricken himself by loss of his own firstborn and heir to the throne. The "passed over" Israeli people set out hurriedly on their march to the land promised to Abraham, Isaac, and Jacob.

Their likely route would take them to the Mediterranean coast and a sure encounter with the Philistines, a militarily able people once colonized by those masters of the sea, the Carthaginians. God chose otherwise and routed them by way of the Red Sea.

This passage foreshadows a constant theme in the history of God's people— "they change their minds." It is never really about war and peace, food or starvation, water or thirst. It is always about whether to trust the one "mighty to save."[87]

> And the LORD went before them by day
> in a pillar of cloud to lead them along the way,
> and by night in a pillar of fire to give them light,
> that they might travel by day and by night.
> The pillar of cloud by day and the pillar of fire by night
> did not depart from before the people.
> (Exodus 13:21–22 ESV)

Some Guide! Some pillars! The Hebrews are about to spend forty years in the hostile environs of the Sinai wilderness. And the one unconfined in time and space takes his place ahead of the troops. Scoutmaster supreme, He condescends to be right there among them in a pillar of cloud by day and a pillar of fire by night. And never did he "depart from before the people."

Who among the most intrepid of us would not balk in fear of a lengthy trek in the desert? Darkness and dryness alone would terrorize and immobilize.

Yet the one "mighty to save" marches ahead in a cloud. Cannot he who resides in the midst of a cloud dispel thirst? The one "mighty to save" blazes the trail in a pillar of fire. Should darkness be feared?

> Then the LORD said to Moses,
> "Tell the people of Israel to turn back
> and encamp in front of Pi-hahiroth,
> between Migdol and the sea, in front of Baal-zephon;
> you shall encamp facing it, by the sea.
> For Pharaoh will say of the people of Israel,
> 'They are wandering in the land;
> the wilderness has shut them in.'
> And I will harden Pharaoh's heart,
> and he will pursue them,

---

[87] Isaiah 63:1.

> and I will get glory over Pharaoh and all his host,
> and the Egyptians shall know that I am the LORD."
> And they did so. (Exodus 14:1–4 ESV)

Trapped! The once *self*-hardened but now *divinely* hardened heart of Pharaoh is jolted into renewed defiance. A final showdown on the banks of the Red Sea will settle the matter once and for all. And there sit the hapless prey—backs to the waters. The fleeing emigrants will be no match for the king's formidable military and six-hundred-plus horses and chariots. Trapped!

Trap! "The Egyptians shall know that I am the LORD." The LORD has been saying exactly that since the beginning contests with Pharaoh. So far, counting the morphing of staffs into serpents, the LORD has pitched an 11–0 shutout. It's extra innings now. But he has in mind a walk-off home run. "I *will* get the glory." When the LORD says, "I *will*," it's safe to predict his opponent "won't." Trap!

> The Egyptians pursued them, all Pharaoh's horses
> and chariots and his horsemen and his army,
> and overtook them encamped at the sea,
> by Pi-hahiroth, in front of Baal-zephon.
> When Pharaoh drew near,
> the people of Israel lifted up their eyes,
> and behold, the Egyptians were marching after them,
> and they feared greatly.
> And the people of Israel cried out to the LORD.
> They said to Moses, "What have you done to
> us in bringing us out of Egypt?"
> (Exodus 14:9–11 ESV)

We aren't told what the people said when they cried out to the LORD. Likely it was something like, "Help." What they said to Moses *is* recorded in all its sarcastic and ingenious creativity. "Is it because there are no graves in Egypt that you have taken us away to die in the wilderness?"[88] Clever! A slave's death in the desert trumps a rebel's drowning in the sea.

Their best bet for human deliverance is to turn 180 degees and begin a long Australian crawl. They have just "lifted up their eyes". They have beheld not the pillar of cloud or pillar of fire, not the ever triumphant I AM. They have beheld their imminent demise at the hands of Pharaoh's army.

"It's you, Moses. You're the problem. Deluded! Daffy! What have you done to us in bringing us out of Egypt?"

> **And Moses said to the people,**
> **"Fear not, stand firm,**
> **and see the salvation of the LORD,**
> **which he will work for you today.**
> **For the Egyptians whom you see today,**
> **you shall never see again.**
> **The LORD will fight for you,**
> **and you have only to be silent."**
> **(Exodus 14:13–14 ESV)**

The concept of "salvation" in the Bible takes a decidedly different slant than "salvation" in any religion or philosophy of life. The gods tell you, "Please me, and I *may* be inclined to lend a hand." Philosophy of life tells you, "There's no such thing as a free lunch" and "What goes around comes around." The I AM's take on salvation is invariably…You are backed against the wall. Maybe it's time to recognize your ineptitude. Or let me put it this way: you are dead in your disability.

In the case at hand, the "wall" is the Red Sea. The situation is hopeless. The people are helpless and as good as dead. So here's the way the I AM routinely does his salvation thing.

---

[88] Exodus 14:11.

Trust me ("fear not").
Don't just do something, stand there ("stand firm").
Watch me do what you can't do
("See the salvation *of the LORD*").
It's not about you, but me
("Which *He* will work *for you* today").

Was that too detailed? Try this. "The LORD will fight for you, and you have only to be silent."

The LORD said to Moses, "Why do you cry to me?
Tell the people of Israel to go forward.
Lift up your staff, and stretch out your hand
over the sea and divide it,
that the people of Israel may
go through the sea on dry ground.
And I will harden the hearts of the Egyptians
so that they shall go in after them,
and I will get glory over Pharaoh
and all his host, his chariots, and his horsemen.
And the Egyptians shall know that I am the LORD,
when I have gotten glory over Pharaoh,
his chariots, and his horsemen." (Exodus 14:15–17 ESV)

In the most bizarre military tactic in all history, the LORD himself commands the people to turn an "about face" from the approaching menace of Pharaoh's army and forward march straight into the sea. A reverse amphibious landing—land to sea. Except the sea won't be there. A dry path between walls of water will mark the route of the would-be Hebrew Marine Corps.

The general's (admiral's?) overall strategy, however, should not be overlooked. This is not ultimately about Hebrews or even Egyptians. It is about the glory of the LORD. Decisive victories are not won by frightened men, women, and children retreating into a separating sea. Nor was this one. It was won by the very creator of the sea. As he once made that sea for his glory alone, he now divides it that even the most powerful of the powerful would know that he is the LORD.

> **Then Moses and the people of Israel**
> **sang this song to the LORD,**
> **"I will sing to the LORD, for he has triumphed gloriously;**
> **the horse and his rider he has thrown into the sea.**
> **The LORD is my strength and my song,**
> **and he has become my salvation;**
> **this is my God, and I will praise him,**
> **my father's God, and I will exalt him.**
> **The LORD is a man of war; the LORD is his name.**
> **Pharaoh's chariots and his host he cast into the sea,**
> **and his chosen officers were sunk in the Red Sea.**
> **The floods covered them;**
> **they went down into the depths like a stone.**
> **Your right hand, O LORD, glorious in power,**
> **your right hand, O LORD, shatters the enemy.**
> **In the greatness of your majesty**
> **you overthrow your adversaries;**
> **you send out your fury; it consumes them like**
> **stubble." (Exodus 15:1–7 ESV)**

Pharaoh's soldiers and charioteers prove no match for the closing waters of the Red Sea. "The LORD has triumphed gloriously; the horse and rider thrown into the sea." Say it once, say it twice, three times. It's the greatest war story of all time. Praise his holy covenant name without ceasing. It is he, not us, who has triumphed gloriously. It is he who is my strength, salvation, and my God. He is a man of war. His right hand, glorious in power, shatters the enemy. His greatness overthrows his adversaries and his fury consumes them like stubble.

In gushing adoration the people of Israel proclaim: "This is my God, and I will praise him, my Father's God, and I will exalt him."

The LORD has his people right where he wants them. Can it last?

Then Moses made Israel set out from the Red Sea,
and they went into the wilderness of Shur.
They went three days in the wilderness
and found no water.
When they came to Marah, they could not drink
the water of Marah because it was bitter;
therefore it was named Marah.
And the people grumbled against Moses, saying,
"What shall we drink?" (Exodus 15:22–24 ESV)

The LORD has His people right where he wants them. Can it last?

For full disclosure of the contents of the Red Sea song of deliverance, see Exodus 15:1–21. Uncontained and long-lasting praise. Lovely! What comes next is related in the verses above and it is not, as they say, "pretty."

We are not told how many times Moses had to hear, "Are we there yet?" We are past that. We now have on our hands a grumpy bunch of amnesiacs who have no memory of the very LORD and Master of the waters. All they know or care about is that they are thirsty. "And the people grumbled."

But the people thirsted there for water,
and the people grumbled against Moses and said,
"Why did you bring us up out of Egypt,
to kill us and our children and our livestock
with thirst?" (Exodus 17:3 ESV)

"Why is the LORD bringing us into this land,
to fall by the sword?
Our wives and our little ones will become a prey.
Would it not be better for us to go back to Egypt?"
And they said to one another,

"Let us choose a leader and go back to Egypt."
(Numbers 14:2–4 ESV)

Here we have the "grumbling" snack pack. Just a sampling of the full-course griping about water, food, and danger.[89] The creative sarcasm at the desperation side of the Red Sea has been eclipsed by simple and direct hostility. "You've got to be trying to kill us. Us and the kids and even the livestock. And what about this I AM in the pillars? Some general he is. We're all going to fall at the swords of our enemies."

The joyous song at the salvation end of the sea had by now been drowned in the "Woe is Me Medley". The wondrous watered greenery of forsaken Egypt has got to be better than this. And they grumbled. Mutiny.

> **Now there was no water for the congregation.**
> **Then Moses and Aaron gathered the assembly**
> **together before the rock, and he said to them,**
> **"Hear now, you rebels: shall we bring water**
> **for you out of this rock?"**
> **And Moses lifted up his hand and**
> **struck the rock**
> **with his staff twice, and water came out abundantly,**
> **and the congregation drank, and their livestock.**
> **(Numbers 20:2, 10–13 ESV)**

Moses' staff, once transformed into a serpent that preyed on other serpents and other staffs, is recalled into service. It had wrought the plagues that ravaged the Nile kingdom. It had separated the waters of the Red Sea.[90] Now it is to summon life-giving water out of a rock.

The trouble, big trouble, lies in the LORD's order to nudge out the water with a tap. Moses, in understandable anger against the rebels and likely in an act of self-validation, bangs on the rock two times in unwitting defiance of the LORD's order to merely speak to and strike the rock. The consequence of disobedience is the denial of Moses' entry into the Promised Land. Small offense, large consequence. If patient, long-suffering, faithful Moses

---

89 See Exodus 16 and Numbers 11 and 20 for more detail on food and water provision.
90 Exodus 14:13–31.

is insufficient to lead the LORD's people all the way from sin and slavery to salvation and security, would there ever be anyone who could? What does God expect? Perfection?

> **And God spoke all these words, saying,**
> **"I am the LORD your God,**
> **who brought you out of the land of Egypt,**
> **out of the house of slavery.**
> **"You shall have no other gods before me.**
> **"You shall not make for yourself a carved image,**
> **or any likeness of anything that is in heaven above,**
> **or that is in the earth beneath,**
> **or that is in the water under the earth."**
> **(Exodus 20:1–4 ESV)**

Unruly, mercurial, and ungrateful, the newly liberated Hebrews had shown little or no inclination to live by the covenant of faith and mutuality established with their ancestor, Abraham. They would require clear moral, legal, and spiritual standards and boundaries. It's time for God to talk.

He does. He calls Moses up Mount Sinai and has much to say. He dictates what would come to be known as the Law of Moses, or just "The Law." This covenant of obedience opens with a list of requirements called the Ten Commandments, the first of which is an absolute prohibition, by the creator of land, sea, and air, of any form of idolatry. The Ten Commandments are followed by lengthy codification of civil, criminal, moral, and ceremonial theocratic law.[91]

Though the demands of the law were rigorous and ultimately beyond human compliance, they are introduced with the tenderness of one who rescues and saves. As Abraham had heard, "I am the LORD who brought you out of

---

[91] The Ten Commandments are found in Exodus 20:1–17 and Deuteronomy 5:4–21. The first five books of the Old Testament are called the Law (Torah). The Torah structured and governed Hebrew theocracy (God rule).

Ur," so his errant descendants are reminded, "I am the LORD your God who brought you out of Egypt, out of the house of slavery."

> **And the LORD said to Moses,**
> **"Go down, for your people, whom you brought up**
> **out of the land of Egypt, have corrupted themselves.**
> **They have turned aside quickly**
> **out of the way that I commanded them.**
> **They have made for themselves a golden calf**
> **and have worshiped it**
> **and sacrificed to it and said,**
> **'These are your gods, O Israel,**
> **who brought you up out of the land of Egypt!'"**
> **(Exodus 32:7–8 ESV)**

While Moses labored on Mount Sinai inscribing the Ten Commandments on two tablets of stone and receiving detailed instruction on the theocratic ways of the covenant LORD God, the people grew frightened and insecure. Surely Moses was a goner. Apparently the pillars of cloud and fire with their other-world inhabitant could no longer be trusted. Let's try the gods of the locals.

Even as the LORD assigned duties for the priestly tribe, Levi, its first high priest, Aaron, was supervising the construction of a golden calf. In the ultimate insult added to injury, the people would not only worship and sacrifice to it, but ascribe to it credit for their delivery out of Egypt.

Moses, on discovery of the aberration, slammed the Ten Commandments to the ground in disgust, destroying them. The golden calf fared even worse. He "burned it with fire and ground it to powder, scattered it on the water and made the people of Israel drink it."[92] Try that water!

> **And the LORD said to Moses, "Write these words,**
> **for in accordance with these words**

---

[92] Recorded in Exodus 32.

I have made a covenant with you and with Israel."
So he was there with the LORD
forty days and forty nights.
He neither ate bread nor drank water.
And he wrote on the tablets the words of the covenant,
the Ten Commandments.
When Moses came down from Mount Sinai, with
the two tablets of the testimony in his hand
as he came down from the mountain,
Moses did not know that the skin of his face shone
because he had been talking with God.
(Exodus 34:27–28 ESV)

While the golden embers yet smoldered, the LORD's divine wrath blazed. Many would pay with their lives for the ultimate of sin—blatant, unapologetic paganism. Not an uninformed worship from the mouths, hands, and knees of blatant, unapologetic pagans but from those the LORD God has named his own—his covenant people.

Punishment follows. Lives abruptly end.[93] The covenant relationship does not. Back up the mountain trudges our octogenarian, Moses. The Ten Commandments are inscribed once again, this time by the very "hand" of God.

Moses started the ascent, having made a most presumptive request. He desired to see his LORD's glory. For forty days and nights, without food and water, he miraculously survives. There's more. The "glory" of the Singular, Eternal, Preexisting, Uncreated Being passes by him, and he lives to tell the story. Would ever again there come such a prophet as this?

After the death of Moses the servant of the LORD,
the LORD said to Joshua the son of Nun, Moses' assistant,
"Moses my servant is dead.
Now therefore arise, go over this Jordan,

---

[93] Recorded in Exodus 33 and 34.

you and all this people, into
the land that I am giving to them, to the people of Israel.
Every place that the sole of your foot will tread upon
I have given to you, just as I promised to Moses.
From the wilderness and this Lebanon
as far as the great river, the river Euphrates,
all the land of the Hittites to the Great Sea
toward the going down of the sun shall be
your territory. (Joshua 1:1–4 ESV)

At age 120, but with neither dimmed eyes nor diminished vigor, Moses trudged up one last mountain. Banned from entering the promised land because of his petulant behavior at Meribah,[94] he was allowed just one longing gaze into the land bounded by the Jordan River. Then, like all before and after him, he died. Many a Christian yet to come would visualize his own passing from life to death and then to life everlasting as "crossing the Jordan River."

For those left behind and under the leadership of Joshua ("the LORD is salvation") "crossing the Jordan" was no figure of speech. The Jordan was the gateway to the entirety of the LORD's Promised Land. At its extremes lay the shores of the vast Great Sea (Mediterranean) and the Great River (Euphrates). Between awaited hostile and well-armed pagan inhabitants in no mood to look askance at trespassers.

JOSHUA

Before the men lay down, she [Rahab] came up to them
on the roof and said to the men,
"I know that the LORD has given you the land, and
that the fear of you has fallen upon us, and
that all the inhabitants of the land melt away before you.
For we have heard how the LORD dried up
the water of the Red Sea before you

---

94 Numbers 20:1–13.

> when you came out of Egypt,
> and what you did to the two kings of the Amorites
> who were beyond the Jordan,
> to Sihon and Og, whom you devoted to destruction.
> As soon as we heard it, our hearts melted, and
> there was no spirit left in any man because of you,
> for the LORD your God,
> he is God in the heavens above and on the
> earth beneath." (Joshua 2:8–11 ESV)

Joshua sent spies into the great, well-armed, and defended city of Jericho, gateway to the Jordan River. In what would become a recurrent surprise in biblical history, a less than prominent or even savory character is used by God to achieve his purposes. It's not a prophet, priest, or king who aids the Israelites. It is a local prostitute named Rahab.

She approaches the spies on the rooftop and tells them what no one else would likely admit. "You guys have wiped out everyone in your path; the Red Sea has been dried before you, and if you want my opinion, the LORD your God has made it all happen, and he is 'God in heaven above and on earth below.'" Rahab tells the spies what they need to know, and she and her family are spared in the destruction to follow—the first among many a "Gentile" (non-Hebrew) to experience the LORD's salvation.

> And as soon as those bearing the ark had come as
> far as the Jordan, and the feet of the priests bearing
> the ark were dipped in the brink of the water
> (now the Jordan overflows all its banks
> throughout the time of harvest),
> the waters coming down from above stood
> and rose up in a heap very far away,
> at Adam, the city that is beside Zarethan, and
> those flowing down toward the Sea of the Arabah,
> the Salt Sea, were completely cut off.
> And the people passed over opposite Jericho.

> **Now the priests bearing the ark of the covenant of the**
> **LORD stood firmly on dry ground in the midst of the**
> **Jordan, and all Israel was passing over on dry ground**
> **until all the nation finished passing over the**
> **Jordan. (Joshua:3:15–17 ESV)**

The "invasion" of lands beyond the Jordan began as the exit from Egypt had ended. Not with armed might but with an awesome miracle. The swollen waters of the Jordan, barring the passage of the LORD God's people, were made to about face and stand at attention while his chosen ones passed through. This time the priests led the way carrying a small chest-like container, the Ark of the Covenant. The ark and its encasing tent of tabernacle represented a visual assurance of the actual presence of the LORD within and about the people.[95]

If Rahab's fellow citizens had reason to tremble behind Jericho's formidable wall before this, they could certainly be excused now for paralysis of courage. First there were those rumored assaults on the Nile so long ago, the separation of the Red Sea, and demolishment of Pharaoh's army. Now the verifiable parting of the Jordan. And the audacity! Priests? The impudent interlopers don't even have the respect to send their soldiers first. Priests!

> **And just as Joshua had commanded the people,**
> **the seven priests bearing the seven trumpets of rams'**
> **horns before the LORD went forward, blowing**
> **the trumpets, with the ark of the covenant**
> **of the LORD following them.**
> **On the seventh day they rose early, at the dawn of day,**
> **and marched around the city**
> **in the same manner seven times.**
> **It was only on that day that they marched**
> **around the city seven times.**
> **So the people shouted, and the trumpets were blown.**

---

[95] Exodus chapters 25–31 detail instructions for building the ark and the tabernacle of the LORD.

As soon as the people heard the sound of the trumpet,
the people shouted a great shout,
and the wall fell down flat. (Joshua 6:8–9, 15, 20 ESV)

Modern kids and adults alike have sung a little ditty called, "Joshua fit the Battle of Jericho, and the walls came tumbling down." Not too much "'fitting" was required to subdue the defenseless, disoriented residents of Jericho. Quaking walls falling down before trumpets and marching priests and civilians doesn't mesh with the average human reason. God's ways seldom do.

Even less logical is why the LORD didn't just say, "Here's home. Settle in." Jericho was then and is now a fabulous oasis with a generous, dependable, massive well. Exactly what manner of city is it that will satisfy this Singular, Eternal, Preexisting, Uncreated Being who inexplicably desires relationship with fallen, sinful people?

"I [the LORD] gave you a land
on which you had not labored
and cities that you had not built, and you dwell in them.
You eat the fruit of vineyards and olive orchards
that you did not plant."
"Now therefore fear the LORD and serve him
in sincerity and in faithfulness.
Put away the gods that your fathers
served beyond the River
and in Egypt, and serve the LORD.
And if it is evil in your eyes to serve the LORD,
choose this day whom you will serve,
whether the gods your fathers served
in the region beyond the River, or
the gods of the Amorites in whose land you dwell.
But as for me and my house, we will serve the
LORD." (Joshua 24:13–15 ESV)

Under Joshua's faithful leadership, the Israelites amassed large chunks of land. As he neared death, he prescribed allotments for each tribe. Here he uses the occasion to remind the people that all this is not their doing. It is an act of amazing, undeserved grace on the part of the I Am, the covenant LORD God of Abraham.

Nor does prosperity come with a never-ending guarantee. The people must decide whether they will serve their savior and provider or serve counterfeits as their parents and grandparents in the land beyond the river and as their pagan neighbors have done between the Euphrates and the Mediterranean. Let's not fake it, gang. It's got to be one or the other. Choose this day whom you will serve! And choose how you will serve. Serve in faithfulness and sincerity. It is, after all, in that manner that the I Am comes to you.[96]

And the people cried out, "No, but we will serve the LORD." We're in. In short time, this was proved otherwise.

JUDGES

> Then the LORD raised up judges,
> who saved them out of the hand
> of those who plundered them.
> Yet they did not listen to their judges,
> for they whored after other gods
> and bowed down to them.
> They soon turned aside from the way
> in which their fathers had walked,
> who had obeyed the commandments of the LORD,
> and they did not do so.
> Whenever the LORD raised up judges for them, the
> LORD was with the judge, and he saved them
> from the hand of their enemies all the days of the judge.
> For the LORD was moved to pity by their groaning

---

[96] Joshua 24.

because of those who afflicted and oppressed
them. (Judges 2:16–18 ESV)

After Joshua came a period, generally marked by appeasement or outright
surrender to the gods of the LORD's sworn enemies. Whether the Israelites
were "whoring" after these gods or opening their bid with flirting, the
LORD justifiably considered it all to be marital infidelity. Yet the rejected
suitor, "moved to pity," intervened repeatedly and compassionately. He
"saved them from the hands of their enemies all the days of the judges."
These judges (intermittent governors) themselves often were far less than
courageous soldiers or even stellar believers. Yet he acted in and through
them. It has always mattered little what the municipal court thinks or does
when the Supreme Court rules otherwise.

The people of Israel did
what was evil in the sight of the LORD,
and the LORD gave them into the
hand of Midian seven years ...
Then Gideon said to God,
"If you will save Israel by my hand, as you have said,
behold, I am laying a fleece of wool on the threshing floor.
If there is dew on the fleece alone,
and it is dry on all the ground,
then I shall know that you will save Israel by my hand,
as you have said."
And it was so. When he rose early next morning
and squeezed the fleece,
he wrung enough dew from the fleece
to fill a bowl with water.
Then Gideon said to God,
"Let not your anger burn against me;
let me speak just once more.
Please let me test just once more with the fleece.
Please let it be dry on the fleece only,
and on all the ground let there be dew."
And God did so that night;

and it was dry on the fleece only,
and on all the ground there was dew.
(Judges 6:1, 36–40 ESV)

Gideon, minding his own business threshing out wheat, received a surprise visit by the "Angel of the LORD." Typecasting for the brief starring role of "judge" consistently came in such a manner. No judge emerged from prestige or previous splendor or acclaim but was called divinely out of the mundane to the seemingly insane—save the people. Since the people had chosen to "displace what was evil in the sight of the LORD" with what was right in their own eyes, God had given them over to the subjection of whatever pagan tribe or nation was at hand.

Gideon responds in a Moses-like attitude pleading all manner of exemption from the draft and eventually lays down a fleece—a test. If you, LORD, tonight saturate this fleece of wool with water leaving the ground dry; if you cover the ground tonight with dew, leaving the fleece dry— "then I shall know that you will save Israel by my hand, as you have said." It is generally shown in the Bible that clear thinkers don't mess with God's head in this or any other such manner. Chalk up Gideon as a rare exception to the rule.

So he brought the people down to the water.
And the LORD said to Gideon,
"Every one who laps the water with his tongue,
as a dog laps, you shall set by himself.
Likewise, every one who kneels down to drink."
And the number of those who lapped,
putting their hands to their mouths, was 300 men,
but all the rest of the people knelt down to drink water.
And the LORD said to Gideon,
"With the 300 men who lapped I will save you
and give the Midianites into your hand,
and let all the others go every man to his home."
(Judges 7:5–7 ESV)

Gideon proves an able army recruiter gathering over 30,000 to face the Baal worshipping Midianites. The LORD chooses otherwise, arranging all but 300 to return home. Twenty thousand of those were dismissed confessing they feared the battle, and ten thousand were mustered out when they kneeled at the water and lapped like dogs. The end is easily predicted. Gideon, the three hundred and the LORD God prove a much more than ample military alliance and Baal and the boys a pathetic foe.[97]

No! But Give Us A King

All the elders of Israel gathered together
and came to Samuel at Ramahand said to him,
"Behold, you are old and your sons
do not walk in your ways.
Now appoint for us a king to judge us like all the nations."
But the thing displeased Samuel when they said,
"Give us a king to judge us."
And Samuel prayed to the LORD.
And the LORD said to Samuel,
"Obey the voice of the people in all that they say to you,
for they have not rejected you, but
they have rejected me from being king over them.
According to all the deeds that they have done,
from the day I brought them up
out of Egypt even to this day,
forsaking me and serving other gods,
so they are also doing to you.
Now then, obey their voice;
only you shall solemnly warn them
and show them the ways of the king who shall
reign over them." (1 Samuel 8:4–9 ESV)

The Hebrew people remained an obstinate and ungrateful lot despite their highlight reel at the Red Sea and their recurrent rescues beyond the Jordan

---

[97] Judges 7 and 8.

by the steadfast and merciful I Am. The period of the judges is approaching an end in these verses. Those neighboring folks and their gods seem to do just fine with kings. But, no, we have to be led by judges!

In the biblical number one out of every "be careful what you ask for, you might get it," the LORD grants their wish. But not without fair warning. A king you shall have, but with him will come war, oppressive taxation, tyranny, and misery. And the people cried out, "No! But there shall be a king over us, that we also may be like all the nations, and that our king may judge us and go out before us and fight our battles."[98]

> **The rest of the deeds of Hezekiah, and all his might,**
> **and how he made the pool and**
> **the conduit and brought water into the city,**
> **are they not written in the Book of the**
> **Chronicles of the Kings of Judah? (2 Kings 20:20 ESV)**

Plenty of water flowed under the Hebrew bridge of history from the establishment of a monarchy under King Saul, its split into two kingdoms (Israel and Judah), the fall of Israel to Assyria in 722 AD, and the demise of Judah in the humiliation of the Babylonian Captivity.[99]

All the longed-for savior kings of Israel and most of those in Judah were tagged Biblically with "he did evil in the sight of the LORD". At the root of the derision was their leading of the people into idolatry. As the last days of the kingdom of Judah neared, a young king named Josiah chose otherwise, restoring and proclaiming the long-ignored and dust-covered Torah, the Law, to the people. Hezekiah earlier had done the same. He also built a tunnel to bring water into Jerusalem. Josiah and Hezekiah, nevertheless, were rare exceptions in a tawdry account of royalty—mere shadows of a lasting and all-encompassing savior king yet to come. The one who would be both the conduit and the essence of living water.

---

[98] 1 Samuel 8.

[99] Babylonian Captivity: Seventy longtime prophesied years of exile after King Nebuchadezzar's Babylonian forces conquered Jerusalem in 586 BC.

KING DAVID AT THE WELL
OF BETHLEHEM

David was then in the stronghold,
and the garrison of the Philistines was then at Bethlehem.
And David said longingly,
"Oh, that someone would give me water to drink
from the well of Bethlehem that is by the gate!"
Then the three mighty men broke through
the camp of the Philistines
and drew water out of the well of Bethlehem
that was by the gate and carried and brought it to David.
But he would not drink of it.
He poured it out to the LORD and said,
"Far be it from me, O LORD, that I should do this.
Shall I drink the blood of the men
who went at the risk of their lives?"
Therefore he would not drink it.
These things the three mighty men did.
(2 Samuel 23:14–17 ESV)

Bethlehem, a seemingly insignificant village about five miles southwest of Jerusalem, cries out "pay attention to me, I'm important," over three hundred times before the Old Testament comes to an end. Jacob's beloved wife, Rachel, is buried there. One of Israel's judges was born there. The book of Judges, itself, is concluded in Bethlehem stories of depravity well capable of shocking the most unshockable, even in our time.[100]

On completion of the book of Judges, the gasping reader who chooses to continue is treated to the book of Ruth, one of ancient literature's great love stories. Ruth, the one-time pagan, is joined in happily ever after matrimony with the devoted Hebrew Boaz. From their union emerges her great-grandson, David. Though King David proves as inadequate as Moses and

---

[100] Genesis 35:19, Judges 12:10, Judges 17–19.

the judges to satisfy the demands of deliverance imposed by the Singular, Eternal, Preexisting, Uncreated Being, one who will follow in his lineage will prove to do just that.

> Then the three mighty men
> broke through the camp of the Philistines
> and drew water out of the well of Bethlehem
> that was by the gate and carried and brought it to David.
> But he would not drink of it.
> He poured it out to the LORD and said,
> "Far be it from me, O LORD, that I should do this.
> Shall I drink the blood of the men
> who went at the risk of their lives?"
> Therefore he would not drink it.
> These things the three mighty men did.
> (2 Samuel 23:16–17 ESV)

> But you, O Bethlehem Ephrathah,
> who are too little to be among the clans of Judah,
> from you shall come forth for me
> one who is to be ruler in Israel,
> whose coming forth is from of old, from
> ancient days." (Micah 5:2 ESV)[101]

In the very town of his birth, King David cried out for water to quench his thirst. When his mighty men return from their perilous quest, he casts it to the ground, revering their dangerous mission and the cost of their blood. The prophet Micah, hundreds of years before the fact, tells of a mightier man, a new king out of Bethlehem—one who will himself through his own sacrifice of blood deliver a living water that never fails in its quenching power.

---

[101] Micah 5:2.

THE BETHLEHEM BABY

Then the angel said to her,
"Do not be afraid, Mary,
for you have found favor with God.
"And behold, you will conceive in your womb
and bring forth a Son,
and shall call His name JESUS.
He will be great, and will be called
the Son of the Highest; and the LORD God
will give Him the throne of His father David.
"He will reign over the house of Jacob forever,
and of His kingdom there will be no end."
Then Mary said to the angel,
"How can this be, since I do not know a man?"
And the angel answered and said to her,
"The Holy Spirit will come upon you,
and the power of the Highest will overshadow you;
therefore, also, that Holy One who is to be born
will be called the Son of God."
(Luke 1:30–35 NKJV)

If current median Bible IQ were to be reduced to one image, one slide show, it may well be that of baby Jesus lying in a manger with proud mom and dad and doting shepherds looking on.

Luke, one of four writers of the New Testament books we call the gospels (good news), recorded that nativity story for all time. He was a doctor by trade and was intrigued by the details of this particular birth and what eyewitnesses and firsthand sources had to say about it.[102] He likely learned that the nine months leading up to the especially blessed day were no more eventful than most others. The child grew in a real womb, likely causing minor and major discomfort to mom throughout the duration. Then, a real baby boy burst through his secure, warm, and watery world,

---

[102] Luke 1:1–4.

squeezing through a painfully restrictive little channel and enduring intense discomfort himself before seeing the light of day.

However, the story begins in an astonishing extraordinary, supernatural manner. An angel appears to a virgin named Mary, announces her pregnancy, reveals the birth of a king whose kingdom shall have no end and directs that the baby be named Jesus (Jehovah is Salvation).

> **Then Mary said to the angel,**
> **"How can this be, since I do not know a man?"**
> **And the angel answered and said to her,**
> **"The Holy Spirit will come upon you,**
> **and the power of the Highest will overshadow you;**
> **therefore, also, that Holy One who is to be born**
> **will be called the Son of God." (Luke 1:34–35 NKJV)**

Doctor Luke takes pains to inform us that this baby is neither the product of egg nor sperm nor a predictable act of birds and bees. "I do not know a man." It is normal water in a real womb that broke that night two thousand years ago. It is no ordinary wet child that emerged but a genuine boy who is true God "conceived by the Holy Spirit, the power of the Highest." The fetching infant of the nativity is none other than Jesus (Savior), the Son of God, the king in the line of David. This is the prophesied child who will rule the kingdom that has "no end."

> **Now the birth of Jesus Christ was as follows:**
> **After His mother Mary was betrothed to Joseph,**
> **before they came together,**
> **she was found with child of the Holy Spirit.**
> **Then Joseph her husband, being a just man,**
> **and not wanting to make her a public example,**
> **was minded to put her away secretly.**
> **But while he thought about these things, behold,**
> **the angel of the LORD appeared to him in a dream,**
> **saying, "Joseph, son of David, do not be afraid**
> **to take to you Mary your wife,**

for that which is conceived in her is of the Holy Spirit.
And she will bring forth a Son,
and you shall call His name JESUS,
for He will save His people from their sins."
(Matthew 1:18–21 NKJV)

Matthew, one of twelve disciples of the adult Jesus, tells the Christmas story from the viewpoint of Mary's fiancé, Joseph. Mr. Nice Guy. His anticipation of wedded bliss has been shattered by a very distressing report. Mary has become "with child." And this she has managed to do without Joseph's participation. Joseph pondered on these things. We are not told how long. Only that his care for her precluded public embarrassment and humiliation. She would be "put away secretly."

Like Mary, Joseph would host an angelic visit, this one in a dream. It's okay, Joseph. "That which is conceived in her is of the Holy Spirit … You will call Him Jesus ['Jehovah is salvation'] for He will save his people from their sins". Another Moses? Another Red Sea? Another Joshua? Another Jordan? Who is it that can wash away sin?

In the beginning was the Word,
and the Word was with God,
and the Word was God.
He was in the beginning with God.
All things were made through him,
and without him was not anything made that was made.
And the Word became flesh and dwelt among us,
and we have seen his glory,
glory as of the only Son from the Father,
full of grace and truth. (John 1:1–3, 14 ESV)

John, one of Jesus's twelve disciples, writing his outlook on Christmas, scrubs the biology and physiology to boldly pen his primary thesis: True God became true man and dwelt among us.

He opens with a thesis statement. The nativity baby of Matthew and Luke is none other than the "in the beginning God" who spoke the universe into existence. The manger newborn was and is God in the flesh.

Inside Mary grew, in fully human form, the Omnipresent, Omniscient, Omnipotent one. Long, long before, when existence was yet confined to Father, Son, and Holy Spirit, he was there. "Earth was yet without form and void." Mary's forming embryo was "I Am" when "darkness was over the face of the deep and the spirit of God hovered over the face of the waters."[103]

> The true light, which gives light to everyone,
> was coming into the world.
> He was in the world,
> and the world was made through him,
> yet the world did not know him.
> He came to his own,
> and his own people did not receive him.
> But to all who did receive him, who believed in his name,
> he gave the right to become children of God.
> (John 1:9–12 ESV)

Having established baby Jesus of Matthew and Luke as the very "in the beginning God" of Genesis 1:1, John brings us back to the big bang itself and identifies the child as "the true light which gives light to everyone." No doubt is left. The Son of God and God himself are one in essence. And as would logically follow, they must be and they are one in purpose. He who created the world from nothing came to bestow a very special right—the right for wayward, rebellious, sinful men, women, and kids to become children of God.

It was and is he, and he alone who is the answer to the question, "Who can wash away my sin?"

---

[103] Genesis 1:1–2, "There is a River."

> Though he was in the form of God,
> He did not count equality with God a thing to be grasped,
> but emptied himself, by taking the form of a servant,
> being born in the likeness of men.
> And being found in human form,
> he humbled himself
> by becoming obedient to the point of death,
> even death on a cross.
> (Philippians 2:5–8 ESV)

The Omnipresent would dwell with man? The Omniscient would willingly embrace the intellect of a newborn? The Omnipotent would suffer the helplessness of a toddler and ultimately of a crucified, condemned criminal? Preposterous!

Preposterous? Not according to John, who testifies to having "seen his glory, glory as of the only Son from the Father, full of grace and truth" and, along with others, having heard, seen, and touched him.[104]

Not according to the apostle (messenger) Paul writing in his book of Philippians. He, attempting to redeem himself "under the law" of perfect obedience to God, had been leveled flat and temporarily blinded on his mission to persecute those who would follow a bodily resurrected savior and lord named Jesus Christ.[105] This Jesus Christ, Paul writes, "in the form of God did not count equality with God a thing to be grasped" but became a servant, a human who would remain obedient to all law, to all love, even to "death on a cross."

> But when the fullness of time had come,
> God sent forth his Son,
> born of woman,
> born under the law,
> to redeem those who were under the law,

---

[104] John 1:3, 1John 1:1.
[105] Acts 9:1–31, Philippians 2:8.

> so that we might receive adoption as sons.
> (Galatians 4:4–5 ESV)

> And it came to pass in those days,
> that there went out a decree from Caesar Augustus,
> that all the world should be taxed.
> (And this taxing was first made
> when Cyrenius was governor of Syria.)
> And all went to be taxed, every one into his own city.
> Joseph also went up from Galilee,
> out of the city of Nazareth, into Judaea,
> unto the city of David, which is called Bethlehem;
> (because he was of the house and lineage of David:)
> To be taxed with Mary his espoused wife,
> being great with child. (Luke 2:1–5 NKJV)

Bible geography expands dramatically with the New Testament and its beginnings in the Christmas story. Far across the Great Sea[106] (Mediterranean Sea), Rome's first emperor, Caesar Augustus, strikes on a wonderful revenue scheme. "I'm going to tax the whole world!"

In "the fullness of time" the Hebrews (Jews) had fallen under the rule of Caesar's sprawling and powerful Roman Empire. And into that fullness arrived Joseph and Mary at Joseph's family city of Bethlehem, the city of King David, to be enrolled for taxation. Here, Mary, sufficiently filled herself, would deliver the Prince of Peace, King of Kings, and Lord of Lords.[107]

Is it true that the only things certain are death and taxes? Augustus is long gone though his legacy as tax collector extraordinaire lives on. Around the world payers are still enrolled, even as early as birth. But he and all the Caesars to follow are extinct. They couldn't beat death. The infant competitor at tax time in Bethlehem was born to do just that.

---

[106] Numbers 34:6. The western boundary of Abraham's promised land.
[107] Isaiah 9:6, Revelation 19:16.

Now when they had departed,
behold, an angel of the LORD
appeared to Joseph in a dream, saying,
"Arise, take the young Child
and His mother, flee to Egypt,
and stay there until I bring you word;
for Herod will seek the young Child to destroy
Him." (Matthew 2:13 NKJV)

King Herod, a puppet local, installed by Caesar to rule over the Jews, took exception to the news that a "king of the Jews" had been born in Bethlehem. He sent out an all-points bulletin ordering the murder of all two-year-old and younger baby boys in that vicinity. Joseph, receiving renewed angelic advice, gathered the wife and child and quickly departed to Egypt.

Once again little Jewish boys are served death warrants by a tyrant king threatened with a rival born to deliver his people. Again the sole survivor will do just that. The first, Moses, freed the slaves, crossed the Red Sea, viewed the Promised Land, and died. The second, Jesus Christ, will enter and leave the land of the Nile, live and die in the Promised Land, then rise from the dead to free the slaves of sin and to live and rule forever.

AT THE JORDAN

In those days John the Baptist
came preaching in the wilderness of Judea,
"Repent, for the kingdom of heaven is at hand."
For this is he who was spoken of
by the prophet Isaiah when he said,
"The voice of one crying in the wilderness:
'Prepare the way of the Lord; make his paths straight.'"
Now John wore a garment of camel's hair
and a leather belt around his waist,
and his food was locusts and wild honey.
Then Jerusalem and all Judea and all the region

> about the Jordan were going out to him,
> and they were baptized by him in the river Jordan,
> confessing their sins. (Matthew 3:1–6 ESV)

Thirty years after the birth of Jesus, the divinely appointed "straight path" of restoration was well under way in the desert wilderness surrounding the Jordan River. Jesus' cousin John,[108] as predicted by the prophet Isaiah, had launched a thriving ministry calling those far and near to confession of sins and to baptism. Clad in little more than Adam and Eve wore when expelled from the garden into their own wilderness, John cried out, "Prepare the way of the Lord; make his paths straight," and, "Repent for the kingdom of heaven is at hand."

Eventually John would run afoul of the law as capriciously laid down by another King Herod.

His head would literally roll.[109] Untimely death, courtesy of capital punishment, would prove to run in the family.

> Then Jesus came from Galilee to the Jordan
> to John, to be baptized by him.
> John would have prevented him, saying,
> "I need to be baptized by you, and do you come to me?"
> But Jesus answered him, "Let it be so now,
> for thus it is fitting for us
> to fulfill all righteousness."
> Then he consented.
> And when Jesus was baptized,
> immediately he went up from the water,
> and behold, the heavens were opened to him,
> and he saw the Spirit of God descending like a dove
> and coming to rest on him;
> and behold, a voice from heaven said,

---

108 Luke 1:5–25, 39–80.
109 Matthew 14:1–12.

"This is my beloved Son, with whom I am well
pleased." (Matthew 3:13–17 ESV)

In the only recorded meeting between the cousins we learn two critical
truths:

1. Jesus, the sinless one, has no need of confession of sins, repentance,
   or a baptism of forgiveness. He, who will humble himself and
   become obedient unto death, here "fulfills all righteousness" and
   sets an example of selflessness for all his followers to come.
2. Eternal Father, eternal Son, eternal Holy Spirit, one God in three
   persons, are together in this "Word became flesh" enterprise. The
   Son's baptism pleases God and in it God declares the oldest love in
   the universe. "This is my beloved son with whom I am well pleased."

IF YOU ARE THE SON OF GOD

Jesus, when he began his ministry,
was about thirty years of age,
being the son (as was supposed) of Joseph,
the son of Heli ... the son of Adam, the son of God.
(Luke 3:23, 38 ESV)

And Jesus, full of the Holy Spirit,
returned from the Jordan
and was led by the Spirit in the wilderness for forty days,
being tempted by the devil.
And he ate nothing during those days.
And when they were ended, he was hungry.
The devil said to him, "If you are the Son of God,
command this stone to become bread."
And Jesus answered him, "It is written,
'Man shall not live by bread alone.'" (Luke 4:1–4 ESV)

Two genealogies of Jesus are presented in the Bible. Matthew bends the family tree back to Abraham, the father of the covenant people of Israel. Luke, more ambitious, links Jesus to Adam, the human father and failure of us all. His gospel leaves no room for doubt of the comparison and contrast.

Luke has promised a friend named Theophilus (friend of God) an "orderly account" of the good news. And what, after all, makes for good news, but the assurance that it displaces bad news. People were meant for paradise, and they botched it. Sin and death had entered the world. Adam had yielded to temptation and to the tempter.

How would a second Adam hold up under the test? Jesus, eternal inhabitant of heavenly wholeness, already having voluntarily deprived himself of divine bliss, rises from the Jordan and treks into the wilderness to endure forty days of starvation.

Enter the Adversary, the ancient serpent, the devil, Satan. Facing temptation, not within the friendly confines of the garden, but in desert deprivation and bodily anguish, Jesus is given an easy out.

You did it before. Do it again. Create. Eat hardy.

Jesus answers with the very words he, eternal God, inspired to be placed in the book of Deuteronomy: "Man shall not live by bread alone." Round one to Jesus. Two ahead. Both conclude with knockdown blows from the same scriptural source. The second Adam is well on the way to defeating sin and death, which the first Adam bought, and restoring the paradise and life that the first Adam squandered.

MINISTRY

**So he came again to Cana in Galilee,
where he had made the water wine.
(John 4:46 ESV)**[110]

---

[110] See full account in John 2:1–11.

Matthew, Mark, and Luke all write of Jesus' baptism in the waters of the Jordan and his resolute and faithful suppression of divine creative powers in the face of desert famish and temptation. The now fully human but always and ever Singular, Eternal, Preexisting, Uncreated Being has created from nothing all that is. Yet he chooses hunger over sin.

At a wedding celebration in a little town named Cana, his mother, Mary, poses a dilemma. "When the wine ran out, the mother of Jesus said to him, 'they have no wine.'" They soon will. The Son of God, though starving, had denied himself a mere loaf of bread. He now transforms twenty to thirty gallons brimful of water into wine. The party may resume. Miracle number one. More to follow, culminating in the greatest of all transformations: death into life.

> From that time Jesus began to preach, saying,
> "Repent, for the kingdom of heaven is at hand."
> While walking by the Sea of Galilee, he saw two brothers,
> Simon (who is called Peter) and Andrew his brother,
> casting a net into the sea, for they were fishermen.
> And he said to them,
> "Follow me, and I will make you fishers of men."
> Immediately they left their nets and followed
> him. (Matthew 4:17–20 ESV)

John had campaigned at the banks of the Jordan River where once God's people crossed into the Promised Land. "Repent," he cried out, "for the kingdom of heaven is at hand." He was, as predicted by the prophet Isaiah, "The voice of one crying in the wilderness, prepare the way of the Lord; make his paths straight."[111]

And now, fresh off his Jordan baptism and desert ordeal, Jesus, too, sounds the marching order, "Repent for the kingdom of heaven is at hand." For twelve men, his disciples, the kingdom of heaven will be as close as Jesus himself for the next three years. Two of them, Jewish fishermen, find a

---

[111] Matthew 3:3.

routine day on the Sea of Galilee, interrupted by a two-word imperative from Jesus: "Follow Me." Astonishingly they do just that. *Immediately.* Peter and Andrew disembark their boat to board the *Good Ship Jesus*, where they will learn to be "fishers of men."

> **Seeing the crowds, he went up on the mountain,**
> **and when he sat down, his disciples came to him.**
> **And he opened his mouth and taught them, saying:**
> **"Blessed are the poor in spirit,**
> **for theirs is the kingdom of heaven.**
> **"Blessed are those who mourn,**
> **for they shall be comforted.**
> **"Blessed are the meek, for they shall inherit the earth.**
> **"Blessed are those who hunger and thirst for**
> **righteousness, for they shall be satisfied.**
> **(Matthew 5:1–6 ESV)**

To the disciples and crowd then and to the world now, the idea that the poor in spirit, the mourning, and the meek are blessed and satisfied seems immeasurably misguided. Miserable, yes! Unfortunate, yes! Blessed? Satisfied? Perish forbid. And the congregation surely murmured, in discordant chorus, "Let's take in a different show" or "more information, please."

Those who stayed seated through the end credits of the three-chapter symposium[112] learned that the key was found in the words "who hunger and thirst after righteousness." Jesus would build his entire ministry exampling service and humility—all for a reason and a motivation that he would hold up for every follower to come. Matthew 5:16 ESV) In the same way, let your light shine before others, *so that* they may see your good works and give glory to your Father who is in heaven.

> **And a great windstorm arose,**
> **and the waves were breaking into the boat,**
> **so that the boat was already filling.**

---

[112] Matthew 5–7.

> But he was in the stern, asleep on the cushion.
> And they woke him and said to him,
> "Teacher, do you not care that we are perishing?"
> And he awoke and rebuked the wind
> and said to the sea, "Peace! Be still!"
> And the wind ceased, and there was a great calm.
> He said to them, "Why are you so afraid?
> Have you still no faith?"
> And they were filled with great fear
> and said to one another,
> "Who then is this, that even
> the wind and the sea obey him?" (Mark 4:37–41 ESV)

One translation[113] renders "asleep" as "sacked out." Jesus was equipped no less than the disciples with all physical and emotional components common to humanity: fatigue, bleeding, sweat, hunger, thirst, energy, anger, compassion, stress, joy, sadness. Here, we see something more—a human oneness with the Father that enables him to rest in a peace that transcends storm. The disciples panic, seeing before them only Davey Jones Locker. Jesus reclines in dreamland. "Do you not care that we are perishing?" He responds. In the same manner in which his primordial words commanded the seas to flow, he demands their retreat. "And there was a great calm." "Even the wind and the sea obey him?" You bet!

> In the fourth watch of the night
> he came to them, walking on the sea.
> But when the disciples saw him walking on the sea,
> they were terrified, and said,
> "It is a ghost!" and they cried out in fear.
> But immediately Jesus spoke to them, saying,
> "Take heart; it is I. Do not be afraid."
> And Peter answered him, "LORD, if it is you,
> command me to come to you on the water."
> He said, "Come." So Peter got out of the boat

---

[113] MIT (idiomatic translation of the New Testament).

and walked on the water and came to Jesus.
When he saw the wind, he was afraid and
beginning to sink he cried out, "Lord, save me."
Jesus immediately reached out his hand
and took hold of him, saying to him,
"O you of little faith, why did you doubt?"
And when they got into the boat, the wind ceased.
And those in the boat worshiped him, saying,
"Truly you are the Son of God."
(Matthew 14:25–33 ESV)

Peter, red-blooded fisherman that he was, likely had spun many a wild story back in the old days. The locals, however, surely balked at the latest. "No, I really did, I walked on water!"

The Bible often leaves out the "why" in its clear presentation of "who, what, where, and when." We are not told why Jesus was strolling on the seas that night. We *are* told the results.

An impetuous disciple got a lesson in faith, as do all who have since named him Lord.

Your pompous and smug self-confidence in calm waters is fatally flawed. I was saving you back then, and it is only I who save when the waters wash over you. It is in the affirmation of his sovereignty over all things, even the raging seas, that all believers must join the disciples in awed confession. "Truly you are the Son of God."

While Jesus was speaking,
a Pharisee asked him to dine with him,
so he went in and reclined at table.
The Pharisee was astonished to see
that he did not first wash before dinner.
And the Lord said to him,
"Now you Pharisees cleanse
the outside of the cup and of the dish,

> but inside you are full of greed and wickedness.
> You fools! Did not he who made the outside
> make the inside also?" (Luke 11:37–40 ESV)

The Pharisees were among the religious elite of their day. They arbitrated, for all, the religious constraints of first century Judaism. Unfortunately their rules and rigors far exceeded the "law" as originally dictated to Moses by the I AM himself.

Centuries before people would wash their bodies and hands on behalf of cleanliness and germ demolition, the Pharisees were washing for show. Super-Jews they were. And Jesus called them on it, identifying them as hypocrites, whitewashed tombs, and blind guides.[114] In this light, "fools" rings charitably. It is the inside Jesus was sent to wash clean. And he would pay dearly for saying so.

> Jesus said to them, "I am the bread of life;
> whoever comes to me shall not hunger,
> and whoever believes in me shall never thirst."
> (John 6:35 ESV)

Once when the Jewish establishment was boasting of its pedigree-- all of them good standing descendants of Abraham who surely outranked Jesus – he responded in no uncertain terms. "Before Abraham was, I am." They took up stones to finish him off.[115] Jesus walked away from this one. But claims of divinity were not to be overlooked. Blasphemy provided far more than adequate grounds for the death penalty.

There's more. He is, or so he claims in a salvo of "I Ams," "the bread of life," "the door," the "good shepherd" and "the light of the world.[116] To a certain woman at a well in neighboring Samaria, he confides that he is "living water." He informs his disciples, on the night before his crucifixion, that he

---

[114] Matthew 15.
[115] John chapter 8 for full account.
[116] John 6:48, John 10:9–16, John 8:12, John 9:5, John 14:6, John 4:10, John 15:5.

is "the way, the truth and the life." Furthermore, he is "the vine," and they "are the branches."

The Pharisees and fellow conspirators had heard more than enough at the Abraham remark and the light of the world quip. Each and every claim invaded the singular sovereignty of the LORD alone. Jesus counts himself as the very Singular, Eternal, Preexisting, Uncreated Being, the One who created all that is from that which had never been? Intolerable!

> **Everyone then who hears these words of mine**
> **and does them will be like a wise man**
> **who built his house on the rock.**
> **And the rain fell, and the floods came,**
> **and the winds blew and beat on that house,**
> **but it did not fall,**
> **because it had been founded on the rock.**
> **And everyone who hears these words of mine**
> **and does not do them will be like**
> **a foolish man who built his house on the sand.**
> **And the rain fell, and the floods came,**
> **and the winds blew and beat against that house,**
> **and it fell, and great was the fall of it.**
> **(Matthew 7:24–27 ESV)**

Spiritual Carpentry for Dummies. "Everyone who hears these words of mine and does them will be like a wise man who built his house on the rock." "Truly, truly, I say to you, whoever hears my word and believes him who sent me has eternal life. He does not come into judgment, but has passed from death to life."[117]

Jesus often spoke in parables—short stories from real life intended to stand alongside and to illustrate an eternal truth. Growing up in the home of

---

[117] John 5:24.

Joseph, the carpenter, [118] he was qualified to speak on the rudiments of construction.

As the "before Abraham was I Am" constructor and sustainer of all things, he was eternally credentialed as the final judge of wisdom and folly. In one of disciple Peter's premier moments, he settled the matter of foolish words and wise words decisively. "Lord, to whom shall we go? You have the words of eternal life." Paul, the greatest missionary of them all tells why. "In Christ are hidden all the treasures of wisdom and knowledge."[119]

> **Again, the kingdom of heaven is like a net**
> **that was thrown into the sea**
> **and gathered fish of every kind.**
> **When it was full, men drew it ashore**
> **and sat down and sorted the good into containers**
> **but threw away the bad.**
> **So it will be at the end of the age.**
> **The angels will come out**
> **and separate the evil from the righteous**
> **and throw them into the fiery furnace.**
> **In that place there will be weeping and gnashing**
> **of teeth. (Matthew 13:47–50 ESV)**

Every Jew living near river or sea would have known food prohibitions on "unclean" sea life and have readily grasped Jesus' warning. "Everything in the waters that does not have fins and scales is detestable to you."[120] The house built on the foundation of fools' words washed away while the one built on solid rock wisdom thrives. So the "good" and the "bad" in the fisherman's net are separated eternally. "Repent for the kingdom of heaven is at hand."

> **Then some of the scribes and Pharisees**
> **answered him, saying,**

---

[118] Mark 6:3.

[119] Colossians 2:3.

[120] Leviticus 11:12.

"Teacher, we wish to see a sign from you."
But he answered them,
"An evil and adulterous generation seeks for a sign,
but no sign will be given to it
except the sign of the prophet Jonah.
For just as Jonah was three days
and three nights in the belly of the great fish,
so will the Son of Man be three days and three nights
in the heart of the earth." (Matthew 12:38–40 ESV)

By the time his earthly ministry was ended, Jesus had fully fed multitudes of five thousand and four thousand on a few fish and loaves of bread, raised three people from the dead, healed the blind, deaf, and lame, and cast out demons. All this in the midst of the most astonishing, transformational, and revolutionary teachings of all time. Yet the religious establishment "wishes" a sign.

Jesus offers but one sign to the "evil and adulterous generation." Remember our prophet Jonah, who was called by God to preach repentance in the wicked Assyrian capital of Nineveh? He fled by boat from the presence of the LORD but could not escape. Tossed into the sea and swallowed by a large fish, he spent three days in its belly before being ejected and sent on to the Assyrian mission field and a victorious season of preaching and salvation.

By implication as clear as Jonah's deliverance, Jesus predicts his death, burial in a tomb, and his bodily resurrection.[121] His mission of triumphant good news and salvation will not be denied, even by death.

"Heaven and earth will pass away,
but my words will not pass away.
But concerning that day and hour no one knows,
not even the angels of heaven,
nor the Son, but the Father only.
For as were the days of Noah,

---

[121] Book of Jonah, Old Testament.

so will be the coming of the Son of Man.
For as in those days before the flood
they were eating and drinking,
marrying and giving in marriage,
until the day when Noah entered the ark,
and they were unaware until
the flood came and swept them all away,
so will be the coming of the Son of Man."
(Matthew 24:35–39 ESV)

Responding to concerns about end-times and how to discern them, Jesus has six things to say. And in reverse order here they are.

6. I, the Son of Man, am returning.
5. Just as it was when floodwaters rose, it will then be too late to worry about it.
4. The last days will look much like the sin-filled days of Noah. "They" will be going about their business—with God as an afterthought or no thought at all.
3. Nobody on earth knows the day or hour, not even the angels or the Son of Man.
2. My words and mine alone are for sure and forever. They *will not* pass away.
1. Heaven and earth *will* pass away.

"There was a rich man
who was clothed in purple and fine linen
and who feasted sumptuously every day.
And at his gate was laid a
poor man named Lazarus, covered with sores,
who desired to be fed with
what fell from the rich man's table.
Moreover, even the dogs came and licked his sores.
The poor man died
and was carried by the angels to Abraham's side.
The rich man also died and was buried,
and in Hades, being in torment,

he lifted up his eyes
and saw Abraham far off and Lazarus at his side.
And he called out, 'Father Abraham,
have mercy on me, and send Lazarus
to dip the end of his finger in water and cool my tongue,
for I am in anguish in this flame.'
But Abraham said, 'Child, remember that you in
your lifetime received your good things,
Lazarus in like manner bad things;
but now he is comforted here, and you are in anguish.
And besides all this,
between us and you a great chasm has been fixed,
in order that those who would pass
from here to you may not be able,
and none may cross from there to us.'"
(Luke 16:19–26 ESV)

In this vivid picture of the consequences of moral and mortal choices, Jesus invokes the imagery of Abraham himself as a potential mediator in the afterlife. The rich man in life had bought far more than fine food and beautiful clothes. For his transactions he now anguishes in waterless poverty while Lazarus, once most miserable of the miserable, reclines in comfort. Abraham addresses the once esteemed but now nameless one. "Child … the chasm is fixed."

THAT YOU ALSO MAY BELIEVE

Jesus, knowing that the Father
had given all things into his hands,
and that he had come from God
and was going back to God, rose from supper.
He laid aside his outer garments,
and taking a towel, tied it around his waist.
Then he poured water into a basin and
began to wash the disciples' feet and to wipe them

with the towel that was wrapped around him.
He came to Simon Peter, who said to him,
"Lord, do you wash my feet?"
Jesus answered him,
"What I am doing you do not understand now,
but afterward you will understand."
Peter said to him,
"You shall never wash my feet." Jesus answered him,
"If I do not wash you, you have no share with me."
Simon Peter said to him,
"Lord, not my feet only
but also my hands and my head!"
(John 13:3–9 ESV)

Here again we find the impetuous but eagerly repentant Peter with his foot in and out of his mouth. It is Thursday, the last night before the agonizing death of Jesus on the cross. He desires to example the life he has come to teach. "If I then, your lord and teacher, have washed your feet, you also ought to wash one another's feet. For I have given you an example, that you also should do just as I have done to you. Truly, truly, I say to you, a servant is not greater than his master, nor is a messenger greater than the one who sent him." (John 13:14–16).

The very God of God and Lord of Lords who humbled himself to become a diapered baby in a manger now washes the desert dust from mortals. Tomorrow he will die for them.

Pilate said to them,
"Then what shall I do with Jesus who is called Christ?"
They all said, "Let him be crucified!"
And he said, "Why, what evil has he done?"
But they shouted all the more,
"Let him be crucified!"
So when Pilate saw that he was gaining nothing,
but rather that a riot was beginning,
he took water and washed his hands before the crowd, saying,

"I am innocent of this man's blood; see to it yourselves." (Matthew 27:22–24 ESV)

Pontius Pilate, the Roman governor in Judea, was in a tricky position. The last thing he wanted was an insurrection in the nation entrusted to him by Tiberius Caesar, the emperor. The Jews had proven a restless lot, politically prone to rebellion and easily agitated over religious issues.

The Pharisees, finally having enough of Jesus, had aligned themselves with other disgruntled members of the powerful ruling religious council, the Sanhedrin. They shared a common purpose: rid themselves of Jesus by any means, including capital punishment, a penalty only the Romans could impose.

Pilate interviewed the accused and proclaimed, "I find no guilt in this man."[122] Not good enough shouted the self-appointed prosecutors, "Let him be crucified." Fearing a riot in the making, Pilate took water and, as we have come to say, "washed his hands of the whole thing."

> **After this, Jesus, knowing that all was now finished,**
> **said (to fulfill the Scripture),**
> **"I thirst."**
> **A jar full of sour wine stood there,**
> **so they put a sponge full of the sour wine**
> **on a hyssop branch and held it to his mouth.**
> **When Jesus had received the sour wine, he said,**
> **"It is finished,"**
> **and he bowed his head and gave up his spirit.**
> **(John 19:28–30 ESV)**

There is not a great deal one is able to say while gasping for breath on a cross of crucifixion. There are only seven recorded sentences from Jesus. [123] We can only bow in awed worship that the he who commanded the king of chemistry, H_2O, into existence must cry out "I thirst."

---

[122] Luke 23:4.
[123] For others, see Matthew 27:46, Mark 15:34, Luke 23:34, 43, John 19:26–27.

And finally the pilgrim of all pilgrims finishes his earthly journey and dies in a foreign land. "It is finished." And just what is "it?" Dying? If it is only dying that he has accomplished, then he is just another "one" among the billions who are destined to achieve exactly the same.

> But when they came to Jesus
> and saw that he was already dead,
> they did not break his legs.
> But one of the soldiers pierced his side with a spear,
> and at once there came out blood and water.
> He who saw it has borne witness—
> his testimony is true,
> and he knows that he is telling the truth—
> that you also may believe.
> (John 19:33–35 ESV)

Jewish authorities petitioned Pilate that the legs of the two criminals being crucified to the left and right of Jesus be broken to hasten their death. The Passover Sabbath day would arrive at dusk, and it would not do to have it defiled by the exhibition of dead bodies outside the holy city of Jerusalem. Pilate consented. Roman soldiers complied. The two received their fatal blows. For Jesus, the measure was unnecessary. He was gone.

One soldier, however, pierced with a spear his lifeless body. From his side spewed blood and water. His disciple John witnessed this and pleaded with all who would read his account to be certain of its truth. Jesus was quite dead. Only blood and water attested to a life now forfeited. For two millennia to come, his followers would proclaim forgiveness of sin through that same shed blood and washing of rebirth in the waters of baptism.

> Now there was a man of the Pharisees
> named Nicodemus, a ruler of the Jews.
> This man came to Jesus by night and said to him,
> "Rabbi, we know that you are a teacher come from God,
> for no one can do these signs
> that you do unless God is with him."

Jesus answered him,
"Truly, truly, I say to you,
unless one is born again
he cannot see the kingdom of God."
(John 3:1-3 ESV)

For God so loved the world, that he gave his only Son,
that whoever believes in him should not perish
but have eternal life.
For God did not send his Son into the world
to condemn the world,
but in order that the world might be saved through him.
Whoever believes in him is not condemned,
but whoever does not believe is condemned
already, because he has not believed
in the name of the only Son of God.
(John 3:16–18 ESV)

A certain Pharisee named Nicodemus had once clandestinely come to Jesus for a little private clarification on what Jesus was all about. What he received up close and personal was twofold:

(1) The mysterious assertion of Jesus that to enter the kingdom of God one must be born again. Enter the watery womb again?

(2) The very good news that eternal life is not dependent on futile religious or otherwise merit but solely on belief in Jesus Christ, the Son of God.[124]

Now on an abysmal black Friday that would eventually be named "Good" stretched in defeat the battered corpse of what had once been for Nicodemus and for the world Hope personified.

---

[124] John 3:1–21 for entire account and John 7:50–53 for Nicodemus's intercession on behalf of Jesus.

PART V

Resurrection to Revelation

They Laid Jesus There

After these things Joseph of Arimathea,
who was a disciple of Jesus,
but secretly for fear of the Jews,
asked Pilate that he might take away
the body of Jesus,
and Pilate gave him permission.
So he came and took away his body.
Nicodemus also, who earlier had come to Jesus by night,
came bringing a mixture of myrrh and aloes,
about seventy-five pounds in weight.
So they took the body of Jesus and bound it in linen cloths
with the spices, as is the burial custom of the Jews.
Now in the place where he was crucified
there was a garden,
and in the garden a new tomb
in which no one had yet been laid.
So because of the Jewish day of Preparation,
since the tomb was close at hand, they laid
Jesus there. (John 19:38–42 ESV)

Adam had begun man's long, recurrently dismal, pilgrimage battered in resounding satanic defeat in the Garden of Eden, the premier well-watered wonder of the world. Jesus began the long trip back to paradise in two lesser but significant gardens.

On the night before his execution he knelt, desperately alone, in the Garden of Gethsemane and prayed that this ordeal, "this cup," might be taken from him. Dr. Luke, writer of the third gospel, ever vigilant for medical footnote, writes that in his agony his sweat "became like great drops of blood falling down to the ground."[125]

Now less than twenty-four hours later, Joseph of Arimathea and Nicodemus, Good Friday's makeshift morticians, laid him to final rest in a garden. Alone he agonized in futility. Alone he died in disgrace. Alone he lay forever. Forever?

It looks that way. And give him credit for flawless prophesy. He had recurrently forecast his imminent death by capital punishment.

But here's the rub. Friend and foe alike also heard with their own ears his audacious prediction of his bodily resurrection. He even forecast the time. The third day.

Sunday!
Sunday to be obscured by time as all the others?
A Sunday to alter the ages?
Which?

HE IS RISEN
HE IS NOT HERE

**If in Christ we have hope in this life only,
we are of all people most to be pitied.**

---

[125] Luke 22:44.

> But in fact Christ has been raised from the dead,
> the firstfruits of those who have fallen asleep.
> For as by a man came death,
> by a man has come also the resurrection of the dead.
> For as in Adam all die,
> so also in Christ shall all be made alive.
> (1 Corinthians 15:19–22 ESV)

> If you confess with your mouth that Jesus is Lord
> and believe in your heart that God raised him
> from the dead, you will be saved.
> For with the heart one believes and is justified,
> and with the mouth one confesses and is saved.
> For the Scripture says,
> "Everyone who believes in him will not be put to shame."
> (Romans 10:9–11 ESV)

"If in Christ we have hope in this life only, we are of all people most to be pitied. But in fact Christ has been raised from the dead." One might expect these seemingly deluded words from one of Jesus' disciples or maybe his mom or a close relative. Instead it was written within very few years of his crucifixion. And by none other than "the Way's" public enemy number one.[126]

Saul, incensed Pharisee extraordinary, had held the coats of those stoning the first Christian martyr, Steven. His rage unspent, he secured permission of the high religious counsel to set out on a search and destroy mission targeting fledgling Christians in Damascus.

However, there on the road to Damascus Saul met the resurrected, ascended, and glorified Jesus. Having departed Jerusalem a voracious bounty hunter, he arrived in Damascus, himself quite bagged—by the living Jesus Christ himself.[127]

---

[126] See Acts 22.
[127] Acts 9:1–31.

Saul, who came to be known as Paul, commenced a 180-degree Godward turnabout. No alteration of his travel lust would be required. The former terror of Christendom was to become "the Way's[128] premier advocate. In three missionary journeys, he would traverse the expanses of the Mediterranean Sea proclaiming throughout the pagan Roman Empire that Jesus Christ had risen bodily from the dead. He lives again. He lives forever. So can you, proclaimed Paul.

> **When the Sabbath was past,**
> **Mary Magdalene, Mary the mother of James,**
> **and Salome bought spices,**
> **so that they might go and anoint him.**
> **And very early on the first day of the week,**
> **when the sun had risen, they went to the tomb.**
> **And they were saying to one another,**
> **"Who will roll away the stone for us**
> **from the entrance of the tomb?"**
> **And looking up, they saw that the stone**
> **had been rolled back—it was very large.**
> **And entering the tomb, they saw a**
> **young man sitting on the right side,**
> **dressed in a white robe, and they were alarmed.**
> **And he said to them, "Do not be alarmed.**
> **You seek Jesus of Nazareth, who was crucified.**
> **He has risen; he is not here.**
> **See the place where they laid him." (Mark 16:1–6 ESV)**

Heavenly messengers (angels) have a habit of startling people. They frequently attempt preemption with "Fear not" or in this case, "Do not be alarmed." In all history it is likely no one needed assurance of calm in the face of perplexity as much as Mary, Mary, and Salome. Consider....

(1) A moment before reaching the tomb, they wondered what gallant men might come forth to roll the stone away. Suddenly they raised eyes to

---

[128] Acts 22.

chivalry satisfied. The stone was indeed rolled away. No sign, though, of the soldiers posted as guard. This must mean trouble of the big-time sort. Or ... maybe they have come to the wrong place.

(2) Not so. Jesus of Nazareth was here, they are assured. *However*—the grave is no longer his home. No corpse here. He is risen. Take a look for yourselves.

It was the first day of the week. The writhing darkness of the bleakest ever Sabbath grudgingly yielded to morning sunshine. Heavenly sunshine. That Sunday morning, that bright first day of the week, has its match only at the first day of creation when the "Spirit of God was hovering over the face of the waters and God said, 'Let there be light,' and there was light."

Now as in the beginning, the Triune God, the three in one, the Singular, Eternal, Preexisting, Uncreated Being, the one who created all that is from that which had never been, teams to repeat the impossible. "He is not here. He is risen."

This Jesus God raised up,
and of that we all are witnesses. (Acts 2:32 ESV)

"For this reason the Father loves me, because
I lay down my life that I may take it up again.
No one takes it from me,
but I lay it down of my own accord.
I have authority to lay it down,
and I have authority to take it up again.
This charge I have received from my Father."
(John 10:17–18 ESV)

If the Spirit of him who raised Jesus
from the dead dwells in you,
he who raised Christ Jesus from the dead
will also give life to your mortal bodies
through his Spirit who dwells in you.
(Romans 8:11 ESV)

For I delivered to you as of first importance
what I also received: that Christ died for our sins
in accordance with the Scriptures,
that he was buried, that he was raised on the third day
in accordance with the Scriptures,
and that he appeared to Cephas, then to the twelve.
Then he appeared to more than
five hundred brothers at one time,
most of whom are still alive,
though some have fallen asleep.
(1 Corinthians 15:3–6 ESV)

On the very day of his resurrection, Jesus was seen by several women, two travelers on the road to Emmaus, and ten of the remaining disciples.[129] Over the forty days prior to his ascension to heaven, he appeared to over five hundred not counting women and children. Within decades, eyewitnesses and the meticulous chronicler, Dr. Luke, were recording his life and times. All their New Testament accounts ended or ultimately centered on the fact and implication of "He is risen." This Paul contends was and is of "first importance." And if you doubt it, he says, check it out. Most of the witnesses are still above ground.

When they [eight disciples] got out on land,
they saw a charcoal fire in place,
with fish laid out on it, and bread.
Jesus said to them,
"Bring some of the fish that you have just caught."
So Simon Peter went aboard and hauled the net
ashore, full of large fish, 153 of them.
And although there were so many,
the net was not torn.
Jesus said to them, "Come and have breakfast."
Now none of the disciples dared ask him,
"Who are you?"
They knew it was the Lord.

---

[129] Luke 24.

**Jesus came and took the bread
and gave it to them, and so with the fish.
(John 21:10–13 ESV)**

On this occasion, during forty days of bodily appearances by Christ before his ascension to heaven, eight disciples led by the ever hyperactive Peter had set out on a fishing trip. Aboard that day was the Missouri disciple,[130] Thomas. He had earlier drawn his line in the sand. Only if his eyes were to gaze on the very wounds of the risen one would he believe. A week later, Jesus presented his punctures and stripes for review and validation. The flabbergasted "doubter" could only offer for the ages, "my Lord and my God." Now on the shores of the Sea of Galilee he, with his angler friends, was to witness the grand finale of resurrection appearances.

Instructed from shore by a mysterious caller to let down their net on only the right side of the boat, they trap 153 of their prey. Not so long ago, Peter and John had run a footrace to the empty tomb. John won. Here's Peter's second chance for athletic glory. "Mysterious caller," my foot! Peter strips down to legitimate swimwear and arrives ashore well ahead of his fellow anglers, who followed dutifully dragging the catch of the ages.

Now they partake of the supreme private dining experience of all time. "My name is Jesus. I have provided your breakfast. It's on me. I'm going to finish cooking it for you now. Oh, and by the way, I'll be your server today."

AROUND THE THRONE

**That which was from the beginning,
which we have heard,
which we have seen with our eyes,
which we looked upon and have touched with our hands,
concerning the word of life—
the life was made manifest, and we have seen it,
and testify to it and**

---

[130] Missouri, the "show me state." See John 20:19–29.

> proclaim to you the eternal life,
> which was with the Father and was made manifest to us—
> that which we have seen and heard
> we proclaim also to you,
> so that you too may have fellowship with us;
> and indeed our fellowship is with the Father
> and with his Son Jesus Christ. (1 John 1:1 ESV)

> Then I looked, and I heard around the throne
> and the living creatures and the elders the
> voice of many angels,
> numbering myriads of myriads
> and thousands of thousands,
> saying with a loud voice,
> "Worthy is the Lamb who was slain,
> to receive power and wealth and wisdom and might
> and honor and glory and blessing!"
> And I heard every creature
> in heaven and in the sea,
> and all that is in them, saying,
> "To him who sits on the throne
> and to the Lamb
> be blessing and honor and glory
> and might forever and ever!"
> (Revelation 5:11–13 ESV)

The disciple John heard and saw plenty in his three years with Jesus. He can barely contain his exuberance to share and to validate his witness. In wrapping up the gospel (Good News) of John, he offers a solemn testimonial to its trustworthiness and adds that if he had reported everything, "I suppose that even the world itself could not contain the books that would be written".[131]

His inadequacy did not stand in the way of his writing four more New Testament books. In the opener, the letter of First John, he pleads the reader

---

[131] John 21:24–25.

to believe his truth—he and others saw, heard, and touched that which is from eternity to eternity. And John just can't keep that to himself. "We proclaim ..." "*so that* you may have fellowship with us." What a fellowship, "leaning on the everlasting arms."[132]

Finally, in the book of Revelation, he relates his exclusive privilege in witnessing a new heaven and new earth immersed in praise for the triumphant Jesus. The perfect Passover lamb, once slain, is eternally alive, well, and victorious. He is worthy!

> **Then I looked, and I heard around the throne**
> **and the living creatures and the elders**
> **the voice of many angels,**
> **numbering myriads of myriads**
> **and thousands of thousands,**
> **saying with a loud voice,**
> **"Worthy is the Lamb who was slain,**
> **to receive power and wealth and wisdom and might**
> **and honor and glory and blessing!"**
> **And I heard every creature**
> **in heaven and in the sea,**
> **and all that is in them, saying,**
> **"To him who sits on the throne and to the Lamb**
> **be blessing and honor**
> **and glory and might**
> **forever and ever!"**
> **(Revelation 5:11–13 ESV)**

The book of Revelation, which concludes the Holy Bible, is centered in a singular three pronged principle:

1. There is, and has been, since the fall of man in the Garden of Eden, a "war in the heavenlies."[133] It may frequently appear that the wrong side is winning.

---

[132] "Leaning on the Everlasting Arms" hymn.
[133] Ephesians 6.

2. Don't ever believe it! Satan appears strong and emboldened today and looked even better on that dark Friday afternoon two millennia ago back in Jerusalem. Don't be fooled by appearances. Satan and those seduced by his works and ways lose. Their conquest is always to the uttermost.

Jesus Christ wins. He wins to the millionth power squared.

Find the sum of that, and then cube it infinitely and eternally. Only then will you have a dim conception of the magnitude of the Lord's victory.

It turns out just as God foretold way back in the third chapter of Genesis. The opening salvo of the great Satan vs. God War was just that—a starter. Momentarily a victory for the challenger, who vanquishes the first Adam. Satan, in the form of a serpent, slithers away in the dust to fight another day. From this point, he dedicates his lifework to displacing God in the minds, hearts, and souls of mankind.

Jesus himself gives him his due. He is "the ruler of this world." Satan is referenced throughout the Bible as a rebellious and fallen angelic being who makes it his business to be the ultimate enemy of both God and man. Scripture identifies him by many names including Satan, Lucifer, the devil, Beelzebub, God of this age, Father of Lies, Murderer, Prince of the power of the air, Man of Sin, Wicked One, and the Tempter. Quite a resume—and nowhere near complete. He is also called a Roaring Lion and by contrast Angel of Light.

So the ultimate question in this war always was, "How will the Ruler of this World fare in mortal combat against the Singular, Eternal, Preexisting, Uncreated Being, the One who created all that is from that which had never been?

**Then I looked, and I heard around the throne
and the living creatures and the elders**

the voice of many angels,
numbering myriads of myriads
and thousands of thousands,
saying with a loud voice,
"Worthy is the Lamb who was slain,
to receive power and wealth and wisdom and might
and honor and glory and blessing!"
And I heard every creature in heaven and in the sea,
and all that is in them, saying, "To him who sits on
the throne and to the Lamb be blessing and honor
and glory and might forever and ever!"
(Revelation 5:11–13 ESV)

Who will triumph in the war to finally end all wars? Who will fall vanquished in the conflagration between the great pretender and the "way, the truth and the life?"[134] How will the ruler of this world fare in mortal combat against the Singular, Eternal, Pre-existing, Uncreated Being, the One who created all that is from that which had never been?

Victory had been sweet, though momentary, for Satan on the battleground of the first garden. How much tastier it must have seemed on that dismal Friday outside the gates of Jerusalem. His thrill of victory[135] could even be celebrated throughout God's special holy day, the Sabbath, and well into the following night and morning. "In your face, God!"

Meanwhile, how is the second Adam doing Friday afternoon? He falls to obscurity and the grave with a mere mighty kick to the heel.[136] Enjoy the early rounds, Satan. Your puny punt to the back foot has heartened you. After all, isn't he dead forever in a donated tomb? Not so. The agony of your defeat awaits only the dawn. It will be your death blow to the head. Your demise may be slow as the world measures time. But it is sure. It is coming.

---

[134] John 14:6.

[135] "Thrill of victory and the agony of defeat" taken from opening to ABC television's *Wide World of Sports*.

[136] Genesis 3:15.

Long ago in that pure garden you polluted every drop of water on earth. You broke the harmony of God's highest creation. Through his existence, man in his new unnatural nature has been out of synch with his God, himself, others, and with creation itself.[137] You are the great disintegrator.

But you've had two thousand years to absorb the truth of ages as recorded in the disciple John's book of Revelation. There awaits for you eternal condemnation. You will go evermore to hell where you belong. You will no longer torment God's own, bought with the precious, perfect blood of his son. But before you go, you will hear what can only be to you an everlasting taunt. You are beat! You are vanquished! Go! Take death with you! And let these words from the LORD's restored creation go with you forever!

> And I heard every creature in heaven and in the sea,
> and all that is in them, saying,
> "To him who sits on the throne and to the Lamb
> be blessing and honor and glory and might forever and ever!"

MULTITUDES WHO SLEEP IN THE DUST

**Daniel was among whom
there was no blemish, but good-looking,
gifted in all wisdom, possessing knowledge
and quick to understand,
who had ability to serve in the king's palace,
and whom they might teach the language
and literature of the Chaldeans.
(Daniel 1:4 NKJV)**

In 586 BC, long before Revelation's drumbeat of victory and defeat, a young boy arrived in Babylon. Daniel was dispatched from Judah by the great and conquering king, Nebuchadnezzar, as part of a program to deliver the best and brightest into his service. What a privilege for an impressionable

---

[137] Bethel Bible Series. *The Bethel Series*, Copyright 1961, 1981, 2000, 2011 by The Adult Christian Education Foundation, Inc., Waunakee, WI, all rights reserved.

adolescent to gaze upon the great Hanging Gardens of Babylon, to bathe in the mighty Euphrates and Tigris Rivers. A far cry from the dry ruins of Jerusalem and its temple where supposedly flowed the "river that makes glad the city of God."

An old song challenged a past American generation when their soldiers came home from World War I: "How are you gonna keep 'em down on the farm after they've seen Paree?"

Would Daniel forsake his God after seeing "Paree?" Would he succumb to the temptations of lavish royal living and pagan seduction? On the contrary. Daniel not only committed himself to be in the world and not of it but so captivated King Nebuchadnezzar that he was made ruler over much of the kingdom. His favor continued with the monarch's Babylonian heirs.

Seventy years later when the empire fell to the powerful Persians, on time as scheduled and prophesied, Daniel continued in office only a short time before displeasing royal power brokers. Bent on destroying him, they presented to King Darius an accurate indictment. This man refuses to abandon worship of his God—despite your orders.

In a distinctly innovative version of capital punishment, Daniel was tossed into a den of lions. His LORD God, in usual and accustomed manner, countered with overwhelmingly superior creativity. While the king, who had never desired Daniel's demise, fasted for a night, so too did the lions, whose stories to their grandchildren must surely have ended with, "Well, shut my mouth." The king woke up to find Daniel well and alive among famished, salivating beasts.

> **"My God sent His angel and shut the lions' mouths,**
> **so that they have not hurt me,**
> **because I was found innocent before Him;**
> **and also,**
> **O king, I have done no wrong before you."**
> **Then the king was exceedingly glad for him,**
> **and commanded that they**

should take Daniel up out of the den.
So Daniel was taken up out of the den,
and no injury whatever was found on him,
because he believed in his God.
(Daniel 12:22–23 NKJV)

Multitudes who sleep in the dust of the earth will awake:
some to everlasting life,
others to shame and everlasting contempt.
Those who are wise will shine
like the brightness of the heavens,
and those who lead many to righteousness,
like the stars for ever and ever. (Daniel 12:2–3 NIV)

Daniel, the aged sage lived on long enough to receive a heavenly forerunner to the book of Revelation—the Old Testament's clearest forecast of life beyond life, of a final reckoning, of glad tidings, and of dire warning.

It's that dust theme again. The LORD God condemned Satan to slither in it. Adam received the devastating news that the only water he could count on was sweat and was informed just where he came from and where he was to return. "In the sweat of your face you shall eat bread till you return to the ground, for out of it you were taken; for dust you are, and to dust you shall return."[138] Abraham pronounced himself "dust and ashes."[139] Job philosophized on rich and poor, able and unable. "They lie down alike in the dust, and worms cover them."[140]

Daniel comes along later to speak of those sleeping in the dust. Sleep in the dust? Good gracious. Stark image. But according to the other guys, it's more. They *become* dust. It's more than they! It's we!

---

[138] Genesis 3:19.
[139] Genesis 18:27.
[140] Job 21:26.

There seems to be no post life underground alternative, including cremation, according to Abraham's self-evaluation as already consisting of "dust and ashes." All end in the same earth and await judgment to glory or to infamy.

Daniel is a great one for the LORD to pick regarding good news of hopelessness turned to hope.

When he arrived in Babylon, all was lost. Seventy years later, the Persians are on the throne, and the king himself has declared that the Jewish captives may return home and even build their temple—on his tab.[141]

Historically, the Hebrew people had a great chance to be a footnote of history. Instead, as good as dead and gone, they are returning home to rebuild their temple and their holy city of Jerusalem.

No small divine intervention. Raising the dead? A different proposition. Yet Daniel uses the illustration of sleeping physical beings, not ghosts or spirits, awakening to renewed life.

Bodily resurrection of the dead to eternal glory or eternal condemnation! What must Daniel have thought? His national heritage was a story of miracles from parting seas to burning waters at the altars of Baal. Yet he offers no detail on this resurrection business. Nor has he any precedents. Five hundred years later, the apostle Paul will have both, and he will wax eloquently on the subject. The mortal dust of his time has been conquered by the "living water" himself, Jesus Christ.

> **Now if Christ is proclaimed as raised from the dead,**
> **how can some of you say that**
> **there is no resurrection of the dead?**
> **But if there is no resurrection of the dead,**
> **then not even Christ has been raised.**
> **And if Christ has not been raised,**
> **then our preaching is in vain and your faith is in vain.**

---

[141] 2 Chronicles 36:22–23. See Isaiah's prediction of this event in Isaiah 44:24–28.

> **We are even found to be misrepresenting God,**
> **because we testified about God**
> **that he raised Christ, whom he did not raise**
> **if it is true that the dead are not raised.**
> **For if the dead are not raised,**
> **not even Christ has been raised.**
> **And if Christ has not been raised,**
> **your faith is futile and you are still in your sins.**
>
> **Then those also who have fallen**
> **asleep in Christ have perished.**
> **If in Christ we have hope in this life only,**
> **we are of all people most to be pitied.**
> **(1 Corinthians 15:12–19 ESV)**[142]

Paul is nearing the conclusion of the first of his two letters to the fledgling Christians in the Greek city of Corinth. There has been trouble in Corinth. Moral issues, confused doctrine, false teachers, and church conflict all have led to disorder and dysfunction. Paul has tactfully but decisively given the church no small dressing down, then added a marvelous description, in chapter thirteen, of the remedy—love. Real love—patient and kind, believing all things, hoping all things, enduring all things.[143]

All this Paul recognizes matters not the least if a certain heresy is not squashed in place. Some in your midst, he says, are proclaiming there is no resurrection of the dead. If that is so, you may as well disregard anything else I or others proclaim as truth. It's all in vain, and so is your faith. You continue to be dead in sin and grandma and grandpa remain confined to the dust.

> **But in fact Christ has been raised from the dead,**
> **the firstfruits of those who have fallen asleep.**

---

[142] See the entire fifteenth chapter of Corinthians for the Bible's richest presentation: bodily resurrection.

[143] 1 Corinthians 13.

For as by a man came death,
by a man has come also the resurrection of the dead.
(1 Corinthians 15:20–21 ESV)

Thus it is written,
"The first man Adam became a living being;"
the last Adam became a life-giving spirit.
But it is not the spiritual that is first
but the natural,
and then the spiritual.
The first man was from the earth, a man of dust;
the second man is from heaven."
(1 Corinthians 15:45–50 ESV)

Back to the Genesis of this whole death saga. It's that dust factor again. The first Adam was created from it and back he went to it. The second scattered it to the winds on the third day.[144]

"In fact," asserts Paul, "He is risen!" The "man of dust" bestows to all the great takeaway—death. The man of heaven counters with grace amazing— his life-giving spirit.

As was the man of dust,
so also are those who are of the dust,
and as is the man of heaven,
so also are those who are of heaven.
Just as we have borne the image of the man of dust,
we shall also bear the image of the man of heaven.
I tell you this, brothers:
flesh and blood cannot inherit the kingdom of God,
nor does the perishable inherit the imperishable.
(1 Corinthians 15:48–50 ESV)

---

144 Genesis 3.

Paul goes on to divide humanity in two. Those allied with the man of dust and those tethered to the man of heaven. As went the first Adam, so go those *of* dust who follow in sin and rebellion. It is more than becoming dust. They *are* dust—waterless, purposeless, and without coherent spiritual substance, destined only to the dust ahead.

The believers in Corinth, they are told, are birthed no better. They bear the image of the doomed man of dust. Like all the rest, without a savior, they enter life a mortal package stamped for death and condemnation. In Jesus Christ the package is indelibly readdressed and sent on its way to heaven. As went the first man of heaven, so go those who follow "by grace through faith." [145]

That being said, Paul has ended his teaching on the men of dust and turns to the highlight of the Good News of Jesus Christ for those "of heaven." Your last breath, ladies and gentlemen, boys and girls, is but the doorway to your breathtaking, imperishable, immortal eternity.

> **I tell you this, brothers:**
> **flesh and blood cannot inherit the kingdom of God,**
> **nor does the perishable inherit the imperishable.**
> **Behold! I tell you a mystery.**
> **We shall not all sleep, but we shall all be changed,**
> **in a moment, in the twinkling of an eye,**
> **at the last trumpet.**
> **For the trumpet will sound, and**
> **the dead will be raised imperishable,**
> **and we shall be changed.**
> **For this perishable body must put on the imperishable,**
> **and this mortal body must put on immortality.**
> **When the perishable puts on the imperishable,**
> **and the mortal puts on immortality,**
> **then shall come to pass the saying that is written:**
> **"Death is swallowed up in victory.**
> **O death, where is your victory?**

---

[145] Ephesians 2:8–10.

O death, where is your sting?"
The sting of death is sin, and the power of sin is the law.
But thanks be to God, who gives us the victory
through our Lord Jesus Christ.
Therefore, my beloved brothers, be steadfast, immovable,
always abounding in the work of the LORD, knowing
that in the Lord your labor is not in vain.
(1 Corinthians 15:51–58 ESV)

And to those Holy Spirit inspired words follow the only fit commentary:
Amen.[146]

AND THEY THREW DUST

And they threw dust on their heads
as they wept and mourned, crying out,
"Alas, alas, for the great city where all who
had ships at sea grew rich by her wealth!"
For in a single hour she has been laid waste.
(Revelation 18:19–21 ESV)

The figurative and representational "great city" of John's end-times Revelation is none other than the Bible's oft revisited Babylon. Here she teams with our old nemesis "dust." It's the last reference for both. How fitting. Death and sin are about to be terminated and dispatched to hell.

Though the great and prosperous city on the Euphrates River had been under dust and ruin for hundreds of years, it yet reigned through the eons as role model for sin, self-will, and self-destruction. The last days Babylonians, citizens of the dust, of vanity, of sin, of idolatry, and of rebellion, can no longer mount a stand. God's wrath has landed in fury.

In an ancient gesture of anguish, they throw dust on their heads, but it is far too late. Their confidence and security embodied in materialism and

---

[146] Amen: "So be it."

ungodliness will lie in waste in but an hour. No more ships. No more rich cargo. It truly is all over but the shouting, and that will not be long.

> **Have this mind among yourselves,**
> **which is yours in Christ Jesus,**
> **who, though he was in the form of God,**
> **did not count equality with God a thing to be grasped,**
> **but emptied himself, by taking the form of a**
> **servant, being born in the likeness of men.**
> **And being found in human form, he humbled himself**
> **by becoming obedient to the point of death,**
> **even death on a cross.**
> **Therefore God has highly exalted him**
> **and bestowed on him the name that is above every name,**
> **so that at the name of Jesus every knee should bow,**
> **in heaven and on earth and under the earth,**
> **and every tongue confess that Jesus Christ is Lord,**
> **to the glory of God the Father. (Philippians 2:5–11 ESV)**

Jesus Christ once had it all and gave it up. Babylon at its best was a slum in contrast to his heavenly home. It is he who is, with the Father and the Holy Spirit, the Singular, Eternal, Preexisting, Uncreated Being. Yet it is he, the one who created all that is from that which had never been, who willingly abandoned it all. And here's the reason. "For you know the grace of our Lord Jesus Christ, that though he was rich, yet for your sake he became poor, so that you by his poverty might become rich."[147]

The man of heaven relinquishes. The man of dust accumulates. The man of heaven empties. The man of dust fills. The man of heaven seeks the sake of others. The man of dust forsakes seeking others.

On Babylon's last day, the judgment is here. Ultimately, every tongue confesses that Jesus Christ is Lord. Every knee bows. If it hasn't happened until now, Babylon, it is far too late.

---

[147] 2 Corinthians 8:9.

BROTHERS WHAT SHALL WE DO?

**Let all the house of Israel therefore know for certain that
God has made him both Lord and Christ,
this Jesus whom you crucified.
Now when they heard this they were cut to the heart,
and said to Peter and the rest of the apostles,
"Brothers, what shall we do?"
And Peter said to them,
"Repent and be baptized every one of you
in the name of Jesus Christ
for the forgiveness of your sins,
and you will receive the gift of the Holy Spirit.
For the promise is for you and for your children
and for all who are far off,
everyone whom the Lord our God calls to himself."
(Acts 2:36–39 ESV)**

Fifty days after the resurrection of Christ, his disciple Peter gave a speech. It turned out to be the inauguration address of the Christian church. Thousands of pilgrims from far and wide were gathered in Jerusalem for the festival of Pentecost. Three thousand of them left the event forever changed. Born again, Jesus called it.[148]

Peter powerfully presented Jesus Christ as the fulfillment of all prophesies. His coming was the plan of the Lord. He is the heir of David who will reign over God's kingdom forever. His death and resurrection were predicted from days of old. And you and the "lawless men" with whom you partnered killed him. He who was sent that those who call on his name may be saved. You crucified him.

"Cut to the heart" by an eternity of truths and indictment, they cried out, "Brothers, what shall we do?"

---

[148] Acts 2 Pentecost Sunday and John 3:3 for Jesus on *born again*.

And Peter answered, "Repent and be baptized every one of you in the name of Jesus Christ for the forgiveness of your sins and you will receive the gift of the Holy Spirit."

And the Holy Spirit saturated soul answered back: (1) I am in sin, big time sin; (2) even big time sin can be forgiven. Even mine. After all, didn't the disciple quote scripture itself[149] as saying those who call on the name of the Lord will be saved?

Three thousand souls having caved to the truth of Pentecost Sunday repented, pivoted 180 degrees from dust to sky, and received the risen Christ as SAVEior.

Good for those folks. They needed a spiritual bath of the first order. Maybe dry cleaning. As for me. I'm getting along just fine. A few blotches, spots, and stains here and there. God is surely pleased with my effort. After all, he wouldn't expect perfection! Would he?

> **"Let all the house of Israel therefore know for certain**
> **that God has made him both Lord and Christ,**
> **this Jesus whom you crucified."**
> **Now when they heard this they were cut to the heart,**
> **and said to Peter and the rest of the apostles,**
> **"Brothers, what shall we do?"**
> **[38] And Peter said to them, "Repent and be baptized**
> **every one of you**
> **in the name of Jesus Christ**
> **for the forgiveness of your sins,**
> **and you will receive the gift of the Holy Spirit."**
> **(Acts 2:36–38 ESV)**

"Brothers, what shall we do?" Fascinating that the crowd having just been reprimanded and shamed would begin its urgent query addressing the disciples as "brothers." The two were certainly in *inadvertent* brotherhood

---

[149] Joel 2:28–32.

two months back. The former condemned Jesus to an emotionally and physically excruciating death, and the latter abandoned him to it.

Things had changed drastically since then. A fraternity of hundreds of true believers had consolidated in the forty days up to the ascension of Christ. Now ten days later in a mighty wash of heavenly waterborne amnesty, the flock swelled by six fold.

But how? "What shall we do?

Hadn't Jesus himself said the way to the kingdom of heaven was narrow and those who find it are few?

This alone left the crowd without hope.

Hadn't Jesus himself commanded, be perfect, as your heavenly Father is perfect?"

Hadn't this left all humanity without hope?

Hadn't the astonished disciples asked, "Then who can be saved" when their teacher proclaimed that it was easier for a camel to go through the eye of a needle than for a rich man to be saved?[150]

After all, even the best of Old Testament prophets and priests understood that only a perfect sacrifice of a perfect animal could atone the cost of sin, even theirs? To try to keep up with that demand tens of thousands of firstborn animals were slaughtered in the annual Passover alone.

Still insufficient.

So what is the answer when the Pentecost three thousand ask, "What shall we do?"

---

[150] Matthew 7:23, 5:48, 19:24.

So what is the answer when the disciples ask Jesus, "Then who can be saved?"

Jesus looked at them and said, "With man it is impossible, but not with God. For all things are possible with God."[151]

> **Let all the house of Israel therefore know for certain**
> **that God has made him both Lord and Christ,**
> **this Jesus whom you crucified.**
> **Now when they heard this they were cut to the heart,**
> **and said to Peter and the rest of the apostles,**
> **"Brothers, what shall we do?"**
> **And Peter said to them,**
> **"Repent and be baptized every one of you**
> **in the name of Jesus Christ**
> **for the forgiveness of your sins,**
> **and you will receive the gift of the Holy Spirit."**
> **(Acts 2:36–38 ESV)**

What shall we do? Who can be saved?

"Be perfect, as your heavenly Father is perfect."

No can do!

Truer words never spoken. We know it. He knows it too.

Jesus already did it for you ... and for us.

We are and always were 100 percent unable.

He is, always was, and always will be, 100 percent able.

> *"With man it is impossible, but not with God.*
> *For all things are possible with God."*

---

[151] Mark 10:26–27.

As for you. Here's what you can and must do.

Repent. Turn from your sins. Turn completely.

Receive in the Holy Spirit and in baptism a new mind, heart, soul and being—a new will locked into *his* very mind, heart, soul and being.

Take and receive what he has already secured and offered to you, the complete forgiveness of all your sins.

There's more, declares Peter, the promise of sin's forgiveness, is extended to the generations.

> **For the promise is for you and for your children**
> **and for all who are far off,**
> **everyone whom the Lord our God calls to himself.**
> **And with many other words he bore witness**
> **and continued to exhort them, saying,**
> **"Save yourselves from this crooked generation."**
> **So those who received his word were baptized,**
> **and there were added that day about three**
> **thousand souls. (Acts 2:39–42 ESV)**

Millions more would follow them into the brotherhood, into the kingdom that has no end.

BABYLON NO MORE

> **"Rejoice over her, O heaven,**
> **and you saints and apostles and prophets,**
> **for God has given judgment for you against her!"**
> **Then a mighty angel took up a stone like a great**
> **millstone and threw it into the sea, saying,**
> **"So will Babylon the great city**
> **be thrown down with violence,**

and will be found no more."
(Revelation 18:20–21 ESV)

Prophets had long been abused by the "Babylonians" of their day. The wicked continually returned their promises of mercy and warnings of judgment with taunts, torture, and termination. Later, within three decades of the resurrection, apostles and saints (believers) would be burning in Rome and being fed to the wild beasts as coliseum entertainment. Millions more have been persecuted and slain for the cause of the good news of Jesus Christ even to our day.

The LORD God, slow to anger and abounding in steadfast love, has finally run his patience to its end. Roles are reversed. He and his church, his holy ones, rejoice in the eternal demise of their unrepentant enemies. All of history's Babylons and Babylonians are symbolically thrown, dragged and anchored forever, to the bottom of the sea to "be found no more forever."

The whole sorry scenario is soon to be much less symbolic and much more specific. The final reality for all who live is not final dust but one of two eternities—the ever-after joyful and glorious fellowship with the LORD God and His people, or the ever-after of despair in their never-ending separation from the LORD God who so desired that all be saved.

THE LORD GOD
DESIRES ALL TO BE SAVED

And I saw the dead, great and small,
standing before the throne,
and books were opened.
Then another book was opened,
which is the book of life.
And the dead were judged
by what was written in the books,
according to what they had done.
And the sea gave up the dead who were in it,
Death and Hades gave up the dead who were in them,

and they were judged,
each one of them, according to what they had done.
Then Death and Hades were thrown into the lake of fire.
This is the second death, the lake of fire.
And if anyone's name was not found
written in the book of life,
he was thrown into the lake of fire.
(Revelation 20:12–15 ESV)

It didn't have to be that way.

For the LORD God] desires all people to be saved
and to come to the knowledge of the truth.
For there is one God,
and there is one mediator between God and men,
the man Christ Jesus,
who gave himself as a ransom for all.
(1 Timothy 2:4–6 ESV)

And just as it is appointed for man to die once,
and after that comes judgment,
so Christ, having been
offered once to bear the sins of many,
will appear a second time,
not to deal with sin but to save those
who are eagerly waiting for him.
(Hebrews 9:27–28 ESV)

Sin has had its day. In the savior's first coming it has lost the battle. It lies writhing at the cross of contempt and the tomb of triumph. In his second it is last seen being flung to the unlimited outer limits. No more sin with which to deal. Only the final verdict for the "eagerly" waiting saints.

Not Guilty
Saved
The Wait Is Over

PART VI

The Dwelling Place Of God

**Then I saw
a new heaven and a new earth,
for the first heaven and the first earth
had passed away,
and the sea was no more.
(Revelation 21:1 ESV)**

Something very new, something not seen since creation is afoot. The ancient skies, earth, and sea, long soiled in censure, give way to new and flawless heirs. Once again all is well in the universe. Even creation breathes a sigh of relief with the closure of a pain and condemnation in no manner self-imposed. This time "it is good" is *for* good.

**For the creation waits with eager longing
for the revealing of the sons of God.
For the creation was subjected to futility,
not willingly,
but because of him who subjected it,
in hope that the creation itself will be set free
from its bondage to corruption
and obtain the freedom of the glory of the children of God.
For we know that the whole creation
has been groaning together
in the pains of childbirth until now.**

And not only the creation, but we ourselves,
who have the firstfruits of the Spirit, groan inwardly
as we wait eagerly for adoption as sons,
the redemption of our bodies.
(Romans 8:19–23 ESV)

All creation joins in the eagerness
and the groaning of God's children

It has been a long, long wait for both.
The anticipation is breathtaking.

Creation, the slave of sin's curse,
Awaits expectantly at the edge of liberty.
She will resume her rightful place in God's order.
Her Genesis spoiler will assume his place also.
A place *made* right by the one who alone is righteous.

And I saw the holy city, new Jerusalem,
coming down out of heaven from God,
prepared as a bride adorned for her husband.
And I heard a loud voice from the throne saying,
"Behold, the dwelling place of God is with man.
He will dwell with them, and they will be his people,
and God himself will be with them as their God.
He will wipe away every tear from their eyes,
and death shall be no more,
neither shall there be mourning,
nor crying, nor pain anymore,
for the former things have passed away."
(Revelation 21:4 ESV)

The Good News knows no end other than the end of tears, death, mourning, crying, and pain. Jesus Christ is descending to earth towing heaven behind. Prepare for the new, better, and best city. Prepare for the new, better, and best wedding and marriage. Prepare for the new, better, and best family. Prepare in triplicate. Father, Son, and Holy Spirit are wrapping it up.

1. *The New Jerusalem.* Earthly Jerusalem, the monotonously failed city of shattered hopes and dreams over which Jesus had wept,[152] is past, to be no more. New Jerusalem, its origins in heaven and its architect the LORD God, is *now* and is scheduled into the *forever.*

   "The loud voice from the throne" declares it so.

2. *The New Matrimony.* Mankind's former and oft broken vow of marital faithfulness, marred by spiritual adultery, separation, and divorce, is past, to be no more. Holy marriage, wedding's perfect match, the Heavenly Father with his beautiful and eternally spotless church bride, is *now* and is scheduled into the *forever.*

   The Singular, Eternal, Preexisting, Uncreated Being
   "The loud voice from the throne" declares it so.

3. *The New Family.* The church militant, separated from the LORD God by mortality, time, and space; brothers and sisters scattered by geography, persecution, division, and death. All are past, to be no more. The church triumphant, family of the LORD God dwelling with man, is *now* and is scheduled into the *forever.*

   The Singular, Eternal, Preexisting, Uncreated Being,
   the one who created all that is
   from that which had never been,
   "The loud voice from the throne" declares it so.

   And he who was seated on the throne said,
   "Behold, I am making all things new."
   Also he said,
   "Write this down,

---

[152] Luke 19:41-42

> for these words are trustworthy and true."
> And he said to me,
> "It is done! I am the Alpha and the Omega,
> the beginning and the end.
> To the thirsty I will give from the spring
> of the water of life without payment.
> The one who conquers will have this heritage,
> and I will be his God and he will be my son."
> (Revelation 21:5–7 ESV)

"It is done." The triumphant words flow from the I AM and from his heavenly throne. Aren't those words a bit familiar? Didn't some mutilated and deluded Roman convict say something like that back in old Jerusalem?

Friday: "It is finished." Out of a trinity of physical, emotional and spiritual anguish, The Son of God slams the gavel on the case of LORD God vs. Death and Sin. Or does he?

Court is in recess until the third day.

Sunday: "Why do you seek the living among the dead? He is not here, but is risen!" Then he said to them, "Thus it is written, and thus it was necessary for the Christ to suffer and to rise from the dead the third day and that repentance and remission of sins should be preached in his name to all nations, beginning at Jerusalem. And you are witnesses of these things."[153]

> Sin: Guilty as charged.
> Sentence: Death
> Publish the verdict
> Final sentence to be rendered
> at a date determined by the Court.

Take notes carefully, John. The Court is not yet adjourned. Tell them. Tell them I am coming in power, judgment, and glory. I am the Alpha and the

---

[153] Luke 24:6, 46–48.

Omega. Share what has been revealed to you. I know not "finished." I know only new beginning. So also will my people. Not I, but "it" was finished when my son spoke past his darkness into my ever-burning light.

My words are trustworthy and true. Spread them to a thirsty people. Take them far. Take them wide. Never stop. One day *it*, death and sin, will be unknown and unuttered. Memory of them will be drowned by the children of the LORD God in jubilant praise of their redeemer. "It is done" will become the choral refrain of an eternity of beginning without end.

"Until then, repentance and remission of sins should be preached in his name to all nations, beginning at Jerusalem. And you are witnesses to these things."

> **And Jesus came and said to them,**
> **"All authority in heaven and on earth**
> **has been given to me.**
> **Go therefore and make disciples of all nations,**
> **baptizing them in the name of the Father**
> **and of the Son and of the Holy Spirit,**
> **teaching them to observe all that I have commanded you.**
> **And behold, I am with you always, to the end**
> **of the age." (Matthew 28:18–20 ESV)**

If you really want to make your point in the ancient Middle East, talk "water." And Jesus did. Right to the end which was a beginning when he, the Singular, Eternal, Preexisting, Uncreated Being, the One who created all that is from that which had never been, cried out for it. "I thirst."

As His days on earth neared their end, he reminded followers and would-be followers of what life in the LORD God is really about. "You shall love! You shall love the LORD your God with all your heart, with all your soul, with all your mind and with all your strength."[154]

---

[154] Deuteronomy 4:29, 6:5, 10:12, 11:13, 13:3, and others; Matthew 22:37.

I have all authority, and I choose to delegate it to you for my glory. I have loved you with an eternal and abiding love. Go therefore and love likewise. You have repented and been baptized in water symbolizing your eternal union with me. Baptize others into the trinity of love, peace and joy. You have learned of my life-giving, soul-filling commands. Teach them. Teach all of them so that men, women, and children may truly live. Go in the name of the Father, and of the Son and of the Holy Spirit and love as I have loved you.[155]

As His days on earth neared their end, he reminded followers and would-be followers of what life in the LORD God is about. "You shall love! You shall love your neighbor as yourself."

> **Then they also will answer, saying,**
> **"Lord, when did we see you hungry or thirsty**
> **or a stranger or naked or sick or in prison,**
> **and did not minister to you?"**
> **Then he will answer them, saying,**
> **"Truly, I say to you,**
> **as you did not do it to one of the least of these,**
> **you did not do it to me.**
> **And these will go away into eternal punishment, but the**
> **righteous into eternal life." (Matthew 25:44–46 ESV)**

And the second great commandment, Jesus said, is like the first. Love! "You shall love your neighbor as yourself." The needy are within your sight, within your reach, and within your ability. Reach to them as I have reached to you. You were not there when I languished in a Roman stronghold, bound and lashed awaiting my appointment with cruel death. You were not there when I hung naked on the cross, estranged from my Father, sick to death in pain, famished and parched.

> I was there for them.
> I was there for you.

---

[155] Leviticus 19:18, Matthew 19:19, Romans 13:9, Galatians 5:14, James 2:8.

I am here for them.
I am here for you.
Reach to me.
Reach to them.

Then God said, "Let there be light;"
and there was light.
(Genesis 1:3 ESV)

A river flowed out of Eden to water the garden,
and there it divided and became four rivers.
(Genesis 2:10 ESV)

And he showed me
a pure river of water of life,
clear as crystal,
proceeding from the throne of God and of the Lamb.
In the middle of its street,
and on either side of the river, was the tree of life,
which bore twelve fruits,
each tree yielding its fruit every month.
The leaves of the tree were for the healing of the nations.
And there shall be no more curse,
but the throne of God and of the Lamb shall be in it,
and His servants shall serve Him.
They shall see His face,
and His name shall be on their foreheads.
There shall be no night there:
They need no lamp nor light of the sun,
for the Lord God gives them light.
And they shall reign forever and ever.
(Revelation 22:1–5 NKJV)

The Holy Bible prefaces its closing, mirroring and often one-upping its opening. In a second and decisive round of perfection the happily ever after surpasses the once upon a time. Darkness itself flickers away to light. The very brilliance of the LORD God. A pure river again springs forth.

Water from the very throne of God and the Lamb.
The Garden blooms anew fed by the pure crystal stream.
This time disease resistant. No more curse.
The Garden is peopled as before.
This time they reign with the LORD God forever and ever.

And the Spirit and the bride say,
"Come!" And let him who hears say, "Come!"
And let him who thirsts come.
Whoever desires, let him take the water of
life freely. (Revelation 22:17 NKJV)

Your mercy, O LORD, is in the heavens;
Your faithfulness reaches to the clouds.
Your righteousness is like the great mountains;
Your judgments are a great deep;
O LORD, You preserve man and beast.
How precious is Your lovingkindness, O God!
(Psalm 36:5–7 NKJV)

There is a river
Whose streams shall make glad the city of God,
The holy place of the tabernacle of the Most High.
(Psalm 46:4 NKJV)

Therefore the children of men put their trust
under the shadow of your wings.
They are abundantly satisfied
with the fullness of your house,
And you give them drink from the river of your pleasures.
For with you is the fountain of life;
In your light we see light.
(Psalm 36:7–9 NKJV)